BRITISH RAILWAYS
WESTERN REGION
in Colour

For the Modeller and Historian

LAURENCE WATERS

Ian Allan
PUBLISHING

CONTENTS

ACKNOWLEDGEMENTS

I would like to thank the following for their help in the preparation of this book: Graham Carpenter, David Castle, Larry Crosier, Tony Doyle, David Hyde, Robin Isaac, Phil Kelley, Doug Nicholls, David Parker, Ron White of Colour-Rail, and the Great Western Trust.

Title page:
Here is a typical scene that lasted almost to the end of steam traction on the Western Region. Merthyr-based (88D) '5700' class 0-6-0PT No 9676 passes Torpantau station on the old Brecon & Merthyr Railway with a pick-up goods service on 3 September 1963. The pick-up was an important feature of many branch and secondary lines, providing supplies for local coal merchants and traders. Here, the train would call at each yard along the route to both pick up or deposit wagons, a time-consuming exercise. Some of these services lasted on some lines long after passenger services were withdrawn, and just like the passenger services before them, lost money. No 9676 was built at Swindon by the Western Region in March 1949 and it carries the later type BR emblem, but is probably still in the original unlined black paintwork that was applied at Swindon when new. It was withdrawn in June 1965. *GWT/MY*

Above:
The 'shape of things to come', so to speak, was the introduction by the Western Region in 1960 of three eight-car 'Blue Pullman' sets. Built by Metro-Cammell, each power car was fitted with a 12-cylinder North British/MAN diesel engine developing 1,000bhp. The units were fitted with Swiss-designed Schlieren bogies to give a better ride. The first of the new air-conditioned trains was introduced between Paddington and Birmingham on 12 September 1960, and eventually, all three sets were employed on services to Bristol, Birmingham and South Wales.

As the name implies, the cars were painted blue, with windows lined in white, and the Pullman crest on the front, but during the late 1960s, the light blue livery was changed to the new BR Pullman grey with yellow ends. The early blue livery can be seen to good effect on the down 'Bristol Pullman' powered by car No W60096 as it speeds throughout West Ealing on 13 February 1962. The 'Birmingham Pullman' was withdrawn in 1967, and after that date, all three sets were used on Paddington–Bristol–South Wales services. The remaining sets were withdrawn from service during 1973. *GWT/CGS*

First published 2005

ISBN (13) 978 0 7110 3146 3

Published by Ian Allan Publishing

an imprint of Ian Allan Publishing Ltd, Hersham, Surrey KT12 4RG.
Printed by Ian Allan Printing Ltd, Hersham, Surrey KT12 4RG.

Code: 0509/C

Visit the Ian Allan Publishing website at
www.ianallanpublishing.com

PREFACE

V. M. Barrington-Ward, a member of the Railway Executive writing in the 1951 report on the 'Unification of British Railways', stated: 'Nationalisation required standardisation of organisation and methods of operating throughout British Railways, and this could not be accomplished without breaking down tradition with a complete recasting of operating practices'.

The Western Region had taken over a tradition that stretched right back to 1838 and Brunel's broad gauge railway. After Nationalisation in 1948, the infrastructure was still pure Great Western and most, if not all, of the workforce were ex-Great Western men. The other regions probably had the same transitional problem, but I think the 'old traditions' survived the longest on the Western Region. The lack of investment, particularly during the early years after Nationalisation, meant the basic infrastructure remained the same

for quite some time. Geoffrey Freeman Allen, in his book *The Western Since 1948*, summed it up when he described the Western Region as the 'Great Western Region'. I would agree with him as I can remember my early trainspotting days in the mid-1950s at Banbury and Oxford, where apart from the intrusion of some BR Standard class engines, Western Region services were still being operated by ex-Great Western steam locomotives, with many trains being formed with ex-Great Western coaching stock.

I have selected pictures that show the Western Region as it was. In many of the illustrations it can be clearly seen just how little the infrastructure inherited by the Western Region from the Great Western, had changed. For the modeller I have tried to show as many different liveries as possible. Obviously, because of the constraints of the book they cannot all be included. The cut-off date for illustrations is 10 June 1986, as on that date the Western Region effectively ceased to exist when the regions were abolished and were replaced by business sectors.

Most of the illustrations are from the Great Western Trust Photographic Collection, which is kept at Didcot Railway Centre. The photographers credited are:

CGS: Charles Gordon Stuart; PAF: Peter Fry; MY: Mark Yarwood; DP: David Parker; JE: John Edgington; KL: Kenneth Leech and KM: K. Marsden.

Below:
Introduced in 1924, the 'Hall' class 4-6-0s worked over the whole system on both passenger and goods services. This class was a direct development of the earlier 'Saints' and was very successful with 349 examples built at Swindon between 1924 and 1950.

On a typical working, No 5951 *Clyffe Hall* is seen here leaving the Frome line at Blatchbridge Junction on 10 June 1962 with the 9.38am service from Cheltenham to Weymouth. Built in December 1935, the engine is running with a later type Hawksworth straight-sided tender. Blatchbridge Junction signalbox was opened on 18 December 1932 and was closed under the Westbury MAS scheme on 13 May 1984. *GWT/PAF*

INTRODUCTION

The 1947 Transport Act, which was introduced by the Labour Government, received Royal Assent on 6 August 1947 and established the British Transport Commission with a remit to run Britain's transport systems. This included the railways, road transport and the ailing canals. The Act nationalised the 'Big Four' main-line railways and some 50 smaller companies into a new Government-controlled British Railways from 1 January 1948.

A second tier of management, the Railway Executive (RE), was formed at the same time and, as its title implies, was responsible for the railways. It is well recorded that for the first few years the two management structures had an uneasy working relationship.

Nationalisation did not result in an immediate cash investment by the government in the new system; in fact, far from it. For many years after Nationalisation, underfunding by successive governments resulted in the railways actually suffering a net disinvestment, an underlying problem that slowed down any form of real modernisation.

Six new regions were formed: the Western, Southern, London Midland, Eastern, North Eastern and Scottish. The new Western Region established its headquarters at Paddington, and inherited some 3,782 route miles of track, hundreds of stations, nearly 4,000 steam and a few diesel locomotives, 130 locomotive depots and sub sheds, a vast amount of passenger and goods rolling stock and thousands of staff from the old Great Western Railway Company (GWR).

The main locomotive and carriage repair works were situated at Swindon, with smaller works at Caerphilly, Wolverhampton, Newton Abbot and Worcester, with a number of smaller repair shops dotted around the system.

One of the first tasks of the new Railway Executive was to introduce regional colour schemes, and a corporate image for locomotives and coaching stock. On the Western this resulted in a brief flirtation with the 'King' class engines being painted in blue, and some 'Castles' in apple green, but this did not last for long and Swindon soon reverted to turning out its engines in Brunswick green. For the Great Western enthusiast of the time this was excellent news; the locomotives were to be retained in what was in effect the old GWR livery. The new corporate livery for station signs etc was brown and cream.

Unlike all the other regions, the Western did not have its locomotives

Below:
Although Nationalisation took place on 1 January 1948, the changeover from the old Great Western Railway Company to the new Western Region did not fully filter through for a number of years. This is well illustrated in this picture taken on 10 September 1949 showing a goods train derailment at Sapperton bank, Gloucestershire. The whole scene is still pure Great Western. The down Paddington to Cheltenham service, which is working wrong line because of the derailment, is in the hands of an unidentified 'Hall' class 4-6-0 in black livery, still with GWR on the tender, the ex-Great Western coaches are in chocolate and cream, and some of the goods wagons still carry private-owner names. *GWT/MY*

renumbered. This was probably due partly to cost rather than sentiment, as the Great Western was the only company to use cast plates rather than painted cabside numbers on its locomotives. Livery on passenger coaching stock was, however, standardised across all six regions, with the introduction of a new 'strawberry and cream' colour scheme.

The RE also looked at the standardisation of upper quadrant signalling across the country, but this also hit the buffers, so to speak, when the Western Region rejected the recommendations and continued to use GWR-design lower quadrant signals. These survived right up until they were replaced by the widespread introduction of multiple-aspect signalling (MAS) from the 1960s. Interestingly, a set of upper quadrant signals had been manufactured at the ex-Great Western signal works at Caversham Road, Reading, during 1950. These new signals were placed, as an experiment, at Oxford North Junction, supposedly in preparation for the introduction of this type of signal on all Western Region routes. However, the Western's resistance to upper quadrants prevailed, and there they remained in solitude until removed in 1973. These were the

only upper quadrant signals in regular use on the Western Region.

The region had also inherited the GWR-designed automatic train control (ATC) system. This was a good, safe emergency system that gave many years of service on the Western Region, but successful though it was, it was not adopted by the other regions, and was eventually replaced by the BR-designed automatic warning system (AWS).

In 1951, the Railway Executive introduced the first of a number of BR Standard design locomotives. The design team was headed by R. A. Riddles, who, prior to Nationalisation, had been the assistant engineer to H. G. Ivatt on the LMS. Riddles had favoured main-line electrification from the word go, but with no government funding forthcoming he designed, instead, a number of 'standard' steam locomotives that would be both easy to service and have the maximum country-wide route availability.

The first of these locomotives were the 'Britannia' class 4-6-2s of which 15 were ordered for the Western Region and were introduced during 1952. Initially, they were used on services to and from the South West, but were apparently not popular with the footplate crews, and within a few years they were all

Above:
The formation of British Railways in 1948 saw a number of ideas put forward for a standard express passenger colour scheme. On the Western Region, during July 1948, four members of the 'King' class (Nos 6001/9/25/26) were painted in an 'experimental' ultramarine blue livery. Eventually, all members of the class were turned out in blue, but this livery was not popular and was soon abandoned in favour of Brunswick green. During this period, all 30 'Kings' were fitted with smokebox numberplates.

The blue livery can be seen to good effect in this view by the late Kenneth Leech of No 6011 *King James I* at Bath Spa in August 1950. The engine is fully lined and has a smokebox numberplate. It is believed the 'Kings' were the first complete ex-GWR class to be fitted with smokebox plates. The tender has the early type 'Wembley' lion-and-wheel emblem. *KL/Colour-Rail/BRW329*

transferred to Cardiff Canton. There, they were used with great success on South Wales express services to and from Paddington.

The BR Standards proved to be successful and between 1951 and 1960 some 12 different classes were constructed comprising a total of 999 locomotives. In 1959, the Western

Region was operating six different classes of BR Standards, totalling 125 locomotives. There has always been a great debate as to whether these locomotives should have been built at all. After Nationalisation, many of the regions, the Western included, were still building steam locomotives to pre-Nationalisation designs. These had been proved over the years and were still ideal for the operation of each region's services. The regions could, and probably should, have continued to operate their own pre-Nationalisation designs, and to extend their working lives until such time that diesel and electric motive power was introduced.

Further changes took place with the introduction of the 1953 Transport Act. This Act abolished the Railway Executive and gave overall control for running the railway to the British Transport Commission under its new chairman, Sir Brian Robertson. The new Act also gave the regions more independence, and in 1956, the Commission allowed each region to introduce some of the old company liveries on a number of main express

services. It was not long before the Western Region used this to great effect. At this time the general manager of the Western Region was K. W. C. Grand. He was a former Great Western man, who prior to Nationalisation had been the assistant general manager of the GWR. It is almost certain that his influence prevailed when a number of new named trains were introduced on the Western during his first year in office, each with sets of the new Mk1 coaches painted in chocolate and cream livery.

For a few years, at least, we had what could be termed an 'Indian Summer' of steam-hauled Western Region express services. Some of these trains, such as the 'Royal Duchy' and the 'Mayflower' served the South West. South Wales was served by the 'Pembroke Coast Express', the 'Capitals United Express' and the 'Red Dragon'. A new Pullman train, the 'South Wales Pullman', had been introduced a year earlier, in 1955.

The 'Cheltenham Spa Express' brought back memories of the pre-war 'Cheltenham Flyer', although the new service was slower. The 'Cambrian Coast Express' and the 'Inter City' ran

Above:
Another interesting, but short-lived livery was light apple green with red and grey lining, seen here on 'Castle' class 4-6-0 No 4091 *Dudley Castle*, again photographed by Kenneth Leech, at Chippenham in 1949. Notice also that the engine is fitted with a brass smokebox numberplate instead of cast iron. Painted on the tender is 'British Railways'. Altogether, nine 'Castles' were turned out in this livery during 1948, but as with the 'Kings' it was soon abandoned in favour of Brunswick green. *KL/Colour-Rail/BRW335*

via High Wycombe and Bicester to Birmingham and beyond. The 'Cathedrals Express' ran from Hereford and Worcester to Paddington and was a personal favourite of mine. Although not a particularly fast service, it called at Oxford en route, and was usually hauled by a clean Worcester-based ex-Great Western 'Castle' class engine.

I was too young to remember the Great Western, but during the 1950s, for all intents and purposes, it was still there for me to see. I am sure many of the staff still considered that they were

Right:
During the early 1950s, the Western introduced the small enamel 'totem' style station names and the larger enamel station running-in boards. However, many of the old Great Western-style wooden station running-in boards survived right up to and beyond the end of steam traction. These boards were generally mounted on cast-iron poles or lengths of redundant rail. A typical example was the wooden board at Castle Cary, seen here on 8 September 1962. It is painted brown with metal letters picked out in cream, and although it shows some damage it is still perfectly usable. *GWT/PAF*

working for the Great Western and not British Railways.

Apart from in the South West, dieselisation was slow to appear on the Western Region, and for a few more years at least, ex-GWR 'Castles' and 'Kings' were still being used on top-link services and continued to be repaired to a high standard at Swindon.

The Modernisation and Re-equipment of British Railways, otherwise known as the 'BR Modernisation Plan', was published in January 1955. The aim of the report was to establish a 'thoroughly modern system', and 'exploit the great national advantages of railways as bulk transporters of passengers and goods'. It was envisaged that it would take some 15 years to implement fully and would cost £1,240 million. The plan included track and signalling improvements, the replacement of steam with diesel and electric traction, new passenger rolling stock, and the remodelling of freight services.

As part of the modernisation plan, MAS was installed between Paddington and Southall during 1956 and was gradually extended westwards, being completed as far as Reading in October 1963, and by 1984, over 800 route miles had been converted.

During 1956, the Western Region started work on the construction of a new station at Banbury. The old station was in a bad state of repair and a replacement was much needed. Rebuilding and track remodelling took a couple of years to complete, and the new station was opened during 1958. Work was also finished at Plymouth North Road. The station was partially reconstructed by the Great Western in 1939, but World War 2 curtailed further work and the rebuilding was not finally completed until 1962 when, on 26 March, it was opened by Dr Richard

Beeching, the then chairman of the British Railways Board.

The introduction of diesel power on the Western Region was also the result of the Modernisation Plan. However, unlike the other regions, which had decided to use diesel-electric motive power, the Western chose to be different, successfully arguing a case for the hydraulic transmission system. This decision was not without foundation, as this system was being used with great success on the Continent, particularly in Germany. The Western based its argument on the success of the V200 diesel-hydraulics of the German Federal Railway, which were introduced in 1953, and were apparently cheap to construct and operate.

Above:
Another example is the wooden running-in board at Builth Road Low Level, pictured on 26 November 1962. The board here has been mounted on sections of redundant rail. With the closure of many stations and the modernisation of others, most of these wooden boards were subsequently burnt. *GWT/CGS*

The Western won the argument and in 1958 five Type 4 diesel-hydraulics were built by the North British Locomotive Company in Glasgow. On 22 August that year, the first of these locomotives, No D600 *Active*, hauled the up 'Cornish Riviera Express' from Penzance to Paddington, and after further testing, all five locomotives were

Above:
Many former broad gauge buildings survived in use, well into Western Region days. A typical example was the goods shed at Wantage Road, seen here shortly after closure, on 17 July 1965. This type of goods shed was used at many locations on the Great Western. Designed by Brunel, the shed at Wantage was constructed of brick with a slate roof, and was opened in the autumn of 1846. It is thought that the small brick lean-to office-type building on the end of the shed was used for a number of years as the station booking office. *GWT/CGS*

put on services between Paddington and the South West. During the same year the first of the Swindon-built Type 4 D800-series 'Warship' class started to appear and after some teething problems soon proved to be more reliable than the North British locomotives, and the Swindon type gradually replaced the latter on services to and from the South West. The Western Region's devotion to diesel-hydraulic motive power saw further types introduced with the North British Type 2s (later Class 22) in 1959, the Beyer Peacock 'Hymek' Type 3s (Class 35) in 1961, the 'Western' Type 4 (Class 52) in 1962, and finally, the Class 14 0-6-0s in 1964. The overall design of the Class 52 'Westerns' was the result of input from the BR Design Panel. This had been set up by the chairman of the BTC, Sir Brian Robertson, in 1956 'to advise on the best means of obtaining a high standard of appearance and amenity in the design of its equipment'. At the time of their introduction and even now, I think the 'Westerns' have a much more modern look about them than the other diesel-hydraulic classes.

The last of the 'Westerns' were delivered in July 1964, but by that time a decision had been made not to order any more diesel-hydraulics for the Western Region and to switch to diesel-electric power. Spares for the North British-built locomotives became a problem after the North British Locomotive Company went into liquidation in April 1962.

The final diesel-hydraulic locomotive to be built at Swindon for BR was Class 14 0-6-0 No D9555 which was completed in October 1965. The Western Region was then operating a total of 365 diesel-hydraulic locomotives. It was sad to see steam replaced, but there is no doubt that the subsequent use of diesel power brought a new era for the travelling public, with cleaner trains and a general increase in train speeds.

The first of the new diesel-electrics, the English Electric Type 3 Co-Co (later Class 37), were delivered to the Western Region in April 1963 and these were followed in December by the Brush Type 4 Co-Co (Class 47). These two classes were soon put to use on both passenger and freight traffic, and in retrospect, one has to question the decision by the Western Region to use diesel-hydraulic motive power as many of the locomotives saw less than ten years' service. The use of diesel-electrics from the start would have proved to be the better option, with a number of Class 37s and 47s still in service some 40 years after their introduction.

Steam traction on the Western Region's secondary services also took a knock with the introduction during 1957 of diesel multiple-units (DMUs). DMUs were first introduced on the Cardiff to Treherbert services on 11 September 1957, to Barry and Rhymney in October 1957, and to all Cardiff Valley services on 13 January 1958. The introduction of diesel traction on Britain's railways was not before time, as by then it was becoming increasingly difficult for all regions to recruit staff for the often arduous and dirty task of servicing and maintaining the steam fleet.

Some early regional boundary changes took place during February 1958, with the Western Region losing some lines and gaining others. Control of the Weymouth area passed to the Southern Region but this was offset by the former Somerset & Dorset line between Bath and Templecombe and the ex-Midland main line between Bristol and Gloucester being placed under the region's control.

During September 1960, an era came to an end, with the withdrawal of slip coach working on the Western Region. Slip coaches had been a major feature of Great Western services since introduction in 1858, but their use declined after World War 2. However, the Western Region still maintained a number of such workings, and in 1958 was slipping coaches from some Bristol services at both Reading and Didcot, and from Wolverhampton services at Bicester. The Reading and Didcot slips were withdrawn at the end of the Summer timetable, on 12 September. This left the Bicester service, which was the very last slip coach working in the country, coming to an end on 9 September 1960. The last slip was made from the 5.10pm fast service from Paddington to Wolverhampton, hauled by 'King' class No 6001 *King Edward VII*. On 12 September 1960, the Western Region introduced the new air-conditioned 'Blue Pullman' service between Paddington, Birmingham and Wolverhampton. Running via High Wycombe and Leamington it was marketed as the 'Birmingham Pullman' and covered the 110-mile journey in just under two hours.

One of the biggest changes to the region came with the publication in 1962 of the *Reshaping of British Railways*, better known as the Beeching Report. Sir Brian Robertson retired as chairman of the BTC in May 1961, and the then Conservative Government appointed Dr Richard Beeching to take his place. Beeching was not a railway man, and had been a technical director of ICI. He was essentially appointed by the government to shake up the system and to cut the constantly rising deficit, which in 1956 stood at £16.5 million and had risen in 1958 to £48.1 million.

In the report, Beeching pinpointed services that were profitable and those that were not. He concluded that in 1961, BR as a whole had 7,000 stations, half of which produced only 2% of the total traffic, and that a quarter of the total traffic receipts were generated by just 34 stations. The appendix of the report listed some 1,928 stations and 266 passenger services nationwide which he deemed should be closed or withdrawn on purely economic grounds, many of course being on the Western Region. The adoption of the report and the subsequent widespread line closures of the mid-1960s effectively changed the Western Region for ever, with counties such as Oxfordshire, Wiltshire, Gloucestershire, Somerset and Devon losing most, and in some cases all, of their branch-line services.

It must be remembered, however, that the Western Region had embarked on the closure to passengers of many unremunerative lines long before Beeching's 1962 report. In South Wales for example, closures included the branches to Cowbridge in 1951, Pontypridd to Llantrisant, and to Ynysybwl in 1952, to Machen in 1956, and from Llantrisant to Penygraig in 1958. On the Brecon & Merthyr the Dowlais branch was closed in 1960, the Merthyr branch in 1961, and the Brecon to Newport line in 1962. Other closures on the Western Region included the branches to Malmesbury, Wiltshire (1951), Faringdon, Oxfordshire (1951), Blenheim & Woodstock, Oxfordshire (1954), Princetown, Devon (1956), Watlington, Oxfordshire (1957) and Moretonhampstead, Devon (1959).

Another part of Beeching's report dealt with the large amount of coaching stock on the system. He concluded that 'passenger rolling stock was excessive for the work load', and 'was expensive to supply, maintain and assemble'. His figures showed that out of a total of 18,500 main-line coaches only 5,500 were in regular use. On the Western Region many of the coaches mentioned in his report were old and had been inherited from the GWR. They were kept mainly for summer excursion traffic and saw little other use. Beeching stated that large numbers of these non-standard coaches were used on average only a dozen or so times a year. His figures indicated a net loss of almost £3 million per year in retaining these vehicles. The implementation of this part of the report saw the widespread withdrawal of this 'surplus' coaching stock, and on the Western Region this resulted in the end for almost all of the remaining pre-Nationalisation coaches.

One positive aspect of the Beeching cuts was that they freed up vital resources that were being bled away by unremunerative lines, and other antiquated working practices, and paved the way for today's modern high-speed passenger railway, and the introduction of the 'Liner' train concept for freight traffic.

The appointment of Stanley Raymond as general manager of the Western Region on 1 January 1962 brought to an end the Western Region tradition of appointing what were essentially former GWR men to this position.

Raymond's task was to reduce the large deficit that the Western Region was accruing each year, and he swept away many of the old traditions and working practices. He, more than anyone, moved away from the 'Great Western Region' syndrome. To do this, he reorganised the traffic management structure with the introduction of four divisions: London, Bristol, Cardiff and Plymouth. Another of his actions was the abandonment of the attractive chocolate and cream livery on coaching stock. It had always been a bit of a problem for the traffic department to ensure that full rakes of this stock were provided for the 'named trains'. Soon, this livery, that had looked so attractive on the BR Mk1 coaches, was phased out in favour of BR maroon. The result was that for a few years' services on the Western Region were formed with coaching stock painted in a variety of colours. In April 1966, this started to change with the introduction by British Rail of a new corporate livery, comprising standard BR blue for all locomotives, and blue and grey livery for coaching stock. The heraldic lion emblem, which had been introduced in 1956, was also dropped in favour of a new double-arrow British Rail logo.

With all of this change going on, Great Western heritage was not completely forgotten and on 23 June 1962, the Great Western Railway Museum at Swindon was opened. Situated in an old railway chapel, the museum initially contained the ex-GWR 'Star' class 4-6-0 No 4003 *Lode Star*, Dean Goods 0-6-0 No 2516, '9400' class 0-6-0PT No 9400, and 'City' class 4-4-0 No. 3440 *City of Truro*. Also on view was the replica broad gauge 2-2-2 *North Star*, together with the 8ft driving wheels from Gooch's 2-2-2, *Iron Duke*.

Further change had taken place with the redefining of regional boundaries on 1 January 1963. These resulted in Western Region lines in the Midlands and North Wales being transferred to the London Midland Region, while Southern Region lines west of Salisbury, together with the Somerset & Dorset line south of Templecombe, passed into Western Region control. Many of these lines were losing money, which did nothing to help the Western Region's own operating deficit, which at this time stood at around £30 million per annum.

The ex-London & South Western Railway (LSWR) main line to Exeter and Plymouth was still marginally a going concern, but the so-called 'Withered Arm' branches to Bude, Ilfracombe, Torrington and Wadebridge, and the South Devon branches to Seaton, Sidmouth and in Dorset, Lyme Regis, were all loss makers, and had little future under the Western Region.

On 6 September 1964, the Western Region introduced a new semi-fast service from Waterloo to Exeter St David's using 'Warship' class diesel-hydraulics, and on the same date, all through services to the North Devon and Cornwall coasts were withdrawn. By 1964, many of the old LSWR branches were being operated with former GWR engines such as '1400' class 0-4-2Ts, '5400', '5700' and '6400' 0-6-0PTs and '4500' class 2-6-2Ts, which had been displaced by DMUs on former GWR services in the South West. This situation did not last for long, as during the next few years passenger services were withdrawn from almost all of the ex-LSWR branches in Devon and Cornwall. The Torrington branch was the first to go, being closed on 4 October 1965, followed by Bude on 3 October 1966, Wadebridge and Padstow on 30 January 1967, and Ilfracombe on 5 October 1970. Lyme Regis lost its passenger services on 29 November 1965, Seaton on 7 March 1966, and to Sidmouth and Budleigh Salterton on 6 March 1967. Today, apart from the ex-LSWR main line from Salisbury to Exeter, only the branches from Exeter to Exmouth, Exeter to Barnstaple, and from Plymouth to Gunnislake, are left of the original LSWR lines taken over by the Western Region in 1963.

It was not just the LSWR lines that were closed during this period. The Western Region also closed a number of ex-Great Western branches in the South West. In Cornwall, only the St Erth to St Ives, the Liskeard to Looe, and the Par to Newquay branches are still in the national timetable. Devon suffered particularly badly with branch-line closures, and today, only the Newton Abbot to Paignton section of the Kingswear branch remains open for passenger services as part of the national network.

Below:
Smiling faces at Colbren Junction on 29 September 1962. Enjoying a joke are the stationmaster, a porter and a couple of guards. They are probably all ex-Great Western men, and even at this date, still had great affection for the old company. The picture was taken from the 11.25am service from Neath Riverside to Brecon. Colbren Junction lost its passenger service just two weeks later, on 15 October 1962. The motorcycle on the platform is a British-built Ariel Leader 250cc two-stroke, a modern British design in 1962. *GWT/PAF*

Four ex-GWR branch lines survive in the South West as preserved railways: the Bodmin & Wenford Railway (Bodmin General to Bodmin Road and Boscarne Junction), the South Devon Railway (Totnes to Buckfastleigh), the Paignton & Dartmouth Railway (Paignton to Kingswear) and the West Somerset Railway (Taunton to Minehead).

In 1965, Beeching produced his second report, The Development of the Major Trunk Routes. This proposed a substantial investment in the development of a 'backbone structure' of main lines. Unfortunately, one of the proposals within the report was for the closure of all lines in Cornwall, the closure of the Berks & Hants 'cut-off route', and the ex-LSWR main line west of Salisbury. If implemented, it would have had a devastating effect on Western Region services. While much of the report made sense, this part was incredibly short-sighted given the growth of road traffic to the South West. Fortunately, protests were loud, and with a number of local MPs together with the Western Region management and the general public resisting the cuts, the threat passed. With much of his job done, Dr Beeching resigned as chairman of the BR Board on 31 May 1965 and returned to his old job at ICI.

Steam was officially withdrawn on the Western Region on 31 December 1965. However, the last official steam service on the region ran on Monday, 3 January 1966 when 'Modified Hall' No 6998 *Burton Agnes Hall* pulled the 14.20 service from Oxford to Newcastle as far as Banbury. This locomotive was purchased just a few days later by the Great Western Society and is now at Didcot Railway Centre.

The removal of steam saw all diesel locomotive maintenance and repair work concentrated at Old Oak Common, Bristol Bath Road, Plymouth Laira, Cardiff Canton, Swansea Landore and, until its closure in 1972, Newton Abbot.

DMU servicing was undertaken at Cardiff, Bristol and Laira, and in the Thames Valley, at Southall, until its closure in November 1986, after which date servicing was switched to a new purpose-built DMU depot at Reading. In later years, separate HST serving facilities were also provided at Bristol St Philip's Marsh, Plymouth Laira, Old Oak Common and Long Rock, Penzance.

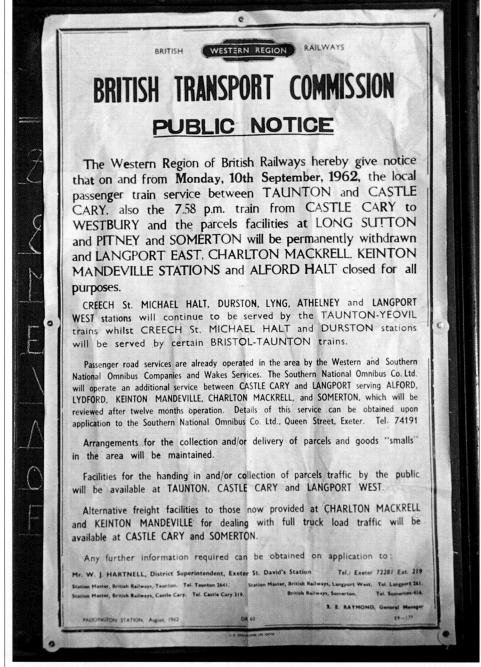

Above:
An all-too-frequent event during the 1960s: a station closure poster, photographed at Castle Cary on 8 September 1962. *GWT/PAF*

By the early 1970s, the remaining diesel-hydraulics were becoming more unreliable and expensive to maintain, and it was during this period that the Western introduced English Electric Class 50s that had been displaced from the West Coast main line. The Class 50s, together with new air-conditioned carriages, were introduced on Western Region services during spring 1974. The end of the diesel-hydraulic era and Swindon's individuality came with the withdrawal of the few remaining 'Warship' Class 42s in 1972, the 'Hymek' Class 35s in 1975, and the 'Western' Class 52s in 1977.

The biggest change to Western Region main-line services occurred with the advent during 1976 of the Class 253 'InterCity 125' High-Speed Trains (HSTs). Their introduction resulted in the upgrading of the main line between Paddington, Bristol and South Wales, and later, the South West. The higher train speeds saw journey times cut, in many cases by a substantial margin.

Brunel's vision all those years ago of a top-quality high-speed railway had come full circle, albeit on the 'wrong' gauge!

The withdrawal of the diesel-hydraulics also had a knock-on effect, as the subsequent loss of repair work meant that the role of Swindon as a major locomotive works diminished. Work now comprised the repair of Class 08 diesel shunters and DMUs and the storage and subsequent cutting up of withdrawn diesels. It was really no surprise when, in 1985, British Rail Engineering Ltd announced the closure of the locomotive works at Swindon, the site subsequently being sold to Tarmac Ltd in 1987. The other two main steam locomotive works on the Western Region had closed some years earlier: the ex-Rhymney Railway works at Caerphilly in June 1963, and the ex-Great Western works at Wolverhampton, Stafford Road in February 1964.

Forward thinking was not one of the strengths of the railway at this time, but the increasing use of the private car for commuting was partially answered by the Western Region with the introduction of a number of Parkway stations. The Parkways were either completely new, or revamped existing stations, each being provided with a large free car park. The first to be opened was Bristol Parkway on 1 May 1972; this was followed by Bodmin Parkway on 1 November 1983, Port Talbot Parkway on 3 December 1984, Didcot Parkway on 19 July 1985 and Tiverton Parkway on 12 May 1986. Sadly, the free parking concept was soon abandoned. The new station at Tiverton adopted a design intended to be used at Hinksey, just south of Oxford. Hinksey Parkway would have been very convenient and would have proved popular with the travelling public, but due to local planning problems it was never built.

The 1980s saw further modernisation and expansion. In Wales, new stations were opened at Cardiff Cathays on 3 October 1983, at Cwmbran on 12 May 1985, and at Lisvane & Thornhill on 4 November 1985. Passenger services were reintroduced between Swindon, Melksham and Westbury on 13 May 1985, having been withdrawn on 18 April 1966. In the South West, a new station was opened at Pinhoe on the ex-LSWR main line east of Exeter, on 16 May 1983.

The line closures of the 1960s and '70s, together with the regional boundary changes, had reduced the Western Region to about half of its size at Nationalisation. By 1980, its route mileage had dropped to just 1,903 miles, serving 493 stations and depots. Main-line motive power was provided by Class 31, 37, 47 and 50 diesel-electric locomotives, InterCity 125s, and a large fleet of DMUs.

Another big change took place in Britain's railway structure, when, on 10 June 1986, the five regions were abolished (the North Eastern having been absorbed by the Eastern earlier), and replaced by new business sectors, including InterCity, Network SouthEast, Regional Railways and Railfreight. The introduction of the sectors saw the end of the BR blue livery period and, in effect, the Western Region as we knew it had disappeared.

However, even today, and nearly 60 years after Nationalisation, it is hard to forget the origins of the railway, with much of the infrastructure from the earliest days of the Great Western still surviving. Brunel's influence can still be clearly seen at stations such as Paddington, Bristol Temple Meads, Frome and Culham, etc, and his major engineering works at Sonning Cutting, Box Tunnel, the Royal Albert Bridge, the Thames Bridge at Maidenhead, and of course the former Great Western main line itself, which is today operated by First Great Western.

Laurence Waters,
Oxford,
2005

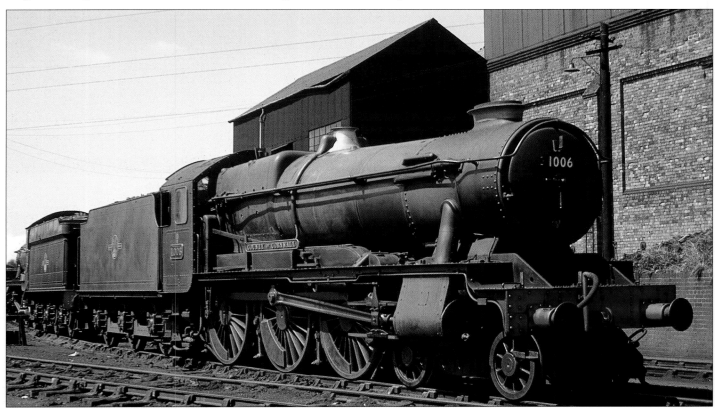

WESTERN REGION STEAM

Ex-GWR steam engines continued to provide much of the motive power for Western Region services, well after the introduction of the new diesel-hydraulics and DMUs during the late 1950s. Steam was to be found all over the system, operating main-line, intermediate, branch and goods traffic. In 1959, some 95% of services on the Western Region were still being operated by steam traction. Dieselisation resulted in the decline of steam, but it was not until 3 January 1966 that the last official Western Region steam working took place when 'Modified Hall' class 4-6-0 No 6998 *Burton Agnes Hall* headed the 14.20 service to Newcastle from Oxford to Banbury. The following selection of pictures illustrate the variety of classes that were still being used by the Western Region well into the 1960s.

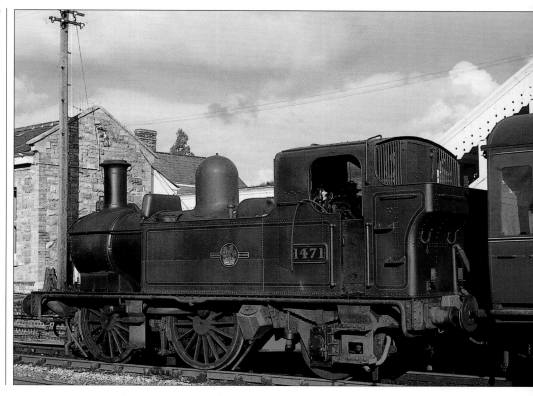

Below Left:
Designed by F. W. Hawksworth in 1945, the 'County' class was the final development of the Great Western 'Saint' class 4-6-0s, and they were the most powerful two-cylinder engines on the GWR and Western Region. Built between 1945 and 1947, they had plate frames and a new, larger No 15 boiler working at 280lb pressure. All 30 engines were fitted with a new-design straight-sided tender. The prototype, No 1000 *County of Middlesex*, was equipped with an experimental double chimney, and between 1956 and 1959, all of the class, including the first, were fitted with double blastpipes and a newer, more squat design of double chimney. The 'Counties' were unusual in having straight rather than curved nameplates, as seen here on No 1006 *County of Cornwall* as it stands at Plymouth Laira on 29 April 1962. The right-hand nameplate was mounted on a raised bracket in front of the reversing lever, but on the left, the plate was mounted directly on the splasher.
CGS/Colour-Rail/BRW1874

Above right:
Introduced by the Great Western in 1932, the Collett '4800' class 0-4-2Ts replaced the ageing '517' class 0-4-2Ts on branch-line services. All were built with automatic train control (ATC) and were auto-fitted. During 1946, the 4800 number series was designated for use on oil-fired locomotives and subsequently the whole class was renumbered as 1400s. From new, they were turned out from Swindon in unlined black, but from 1956 many were painted in fully lined BR Brunswick green, as can be seen on No 1471 as it stands at Dulverton on 15 November 1962 with an afternoon arrival from Tiverton. The engine is fitted with top-feed apparatus, but not all of the class were so fitted. No 1471 was withdrawn from service in October 1963. *GWT/CGS*

Below:
A number of the auto trailer coaches had been converted from steam railmotors by the GWR, while others were converted from ordinary coaches. By the early 1950s, some of the older auto trailers were worn out and in 1951 the Western Region constructed 15 replacements for branch-line services. The new coaches, not unsurprisingly were built to a GWR saloon-type design but with modern sliding ventilators to the windows. The intention was to name them after British birds, but only two were so treated: Nos W220W *Thrush* and W221W *Wren*. The first is seen here at Dulverton after arriving on a service from Tiverton on 15 November 1962. The second coach is an ex-GWR Collett non-Corridor Brake Third; both are painted in BR maroon livery.
GWT/CGS

Above:

Another auto train service, comprising two auto coaches and '1400' class 0-4-2T No 1473, passes the ex-broad gauge goods shed at Stroud with the 6.3pm service from Chalford to Gloucester Central, on 14 July 1962. The driver is controlling the train from the front auto coach. The stone goods shed and tall office building date from around the opening of the line by the GWR on 12 May 1845. The building is now listed and has recently been restored. Chalford to Gloucester was one of the last auto services to operate on the Western Region, the service being withdrawn as a result of the Beeching cuts, on 2 November 1964. *GWT/PAF*

Right:

The 10 '1500' class 0-6-0PTs were different from the usual GW design in that they had no running plates as such, and although built to a smaller wheelbase, were actually heavier than other Great Western-design 0-6-0PTs. The class was designed by Hawksworth, but built by BR at Swindon in 1949. The first five engines were used on empty carriage duties in and out of Paddington, with the other five based in South Wales where they were used for yard shunting. Receiving some attention at Old Oak Common on 11 March 1962 is No 1504. The lack of a running plate made maintenance that much easier. No 1504, seen here in standard BR black livery, was withdrawn from Old Oak Common in May 1963. *GWT/CGS*

Right:
Several ex-Great Western 0-6-0PTs were fitted with spark arresting chimneys for working in areas where there may have been a fire risk, such as factories or works sidings. Pictured here at Worcester on 23 July 1962, is '1600' class 0-6-0PT No 1661, one of only three members of the class to be fitted with such a chimney. The '1600s' were designed by Hawksworth for light branch-line and shunting duties, but all 70 members of the class were built after Nationalisation. A feature of the design was a reduced loading gauge which allowed them to work over routes with low overbridges and restricted clearance. No 1661 was one of the final batch built, being turned out from Swindon in March 1955 and is seen here painted in unlined black and still retaining the early style lion and wheel emblem. It had a relatively short life and was withdrawn in July 1964. *GWT/CGS*

Above:
A '2251' class 0-6-0, No 2298, in plain black livery stands in the bay platform at Brecon with an afternoon service to Newport on 26 November 1962. This class was designed by Collett in 1930 to replace some of the older 0-6-0s that were becoming life expired. The '2251s' were useful engines, of which 120 were constructed at Swindon between 1930 and 1948, all passing into Western Region ownership. They worked on a variety of services including intermediate and branch passenger trains, and also goods services. The whole class was originally turned out in standard black livery, but from 1957, a number were painted in BR lined green. No 2298 was withdrawn in December 1963. *GWT/CGS*

Above:

The Churchward '2800' class were the first 2-8-0s to be introduced in this country and were the mainstay of heavy goods services on both the Great Western Railway and the Western Region. The first batch of 84 engines were constructed between 1903 and 1919, with a further 83 built between 1938 and 1942. These latter engines were designated '2884' class and had a number of alterations including outside steam pipes and side-window cabs. Passing through Tiverton Junction with a westbound goods service on 15 November 1962 is rather grubby-looking '2884' class No 3838. The engine carries an 86E Severn Tunnel Junction shedplate and is in unlined black livery. Built at Swindon in January 1942, it was withdrawn in November 1964. The Western Region first introduced smokebox door shed code plates during February 1950. *GWT/CGS*

Left:

Looking superb in BR unlined Brunswick green is '5101' class 2-6-2T No 4100 as it stands at Gloucester Central on 13 April 1962 with a service from Hereford. The '5101s' were constructed between 1929 and 1949, essentially for suburban and branch-line use. No 4100 was built at Swindon in August 1935 and was withdrawn in October 1965. The four-coach train comprises ex-Great Western stock in both maroon and 'strawberry and cream' liveries; next to the locomotive is Collett Corridor all-Third No W5768W. *GWT/CGS*

Right:

Standing at Bodmin Road with a service to Wadebridge on 27 April 1962 is '4575' class 2-6-2T No 5518. Designed by Churchward for light branch work, the '4500/4575' classes saw extensive use on many branch lines over the whole system, and particularly in the South West. From about 1957, and as they went through the works, many of the class were repainted in BR lined-green livery. No 5518 is however still in black livery with the early type BR emblem and an 83C Exeter shedplate. The '4575s' differed from the earlier '4500s' in having larger, tapered side tanks. No 5518 was withdrawn from service in May 1964. *GWT/CGS*

Above:

While the 'Kings' hauled the heaviest trains on the Western Region, it would be true to say that the 'Castles' hauled the fastest. The 'Castles' had evolved from Churchward's 'Star' class 4-6-0s, which were designed in 1906. Collett improved on Churchward's design with the addition of a larger boiler which helped to increase the tractive effort. The result was that the 'Castle' 4-6-0s were probably the best all-round express passenger locomotives in the country. First introduced in 1923, some 167 were built from new or converted from 'Stars'. The last 30 'Castles' were actually constructed by British Railways,

between 1948 and 1950. From May 1956, 66 members of the class had their performance improved when they were fitted with four-row superheaters and double chimneys.

Waiting to depart from Oxford on 10 August 1962 with the 5.35pm non-stop service to Paddington is No 4089 *Donnington Castle*. The six coaches were a regular load for this service. The engine still has a single chimney, but is coupled to a later type Hawksworth straight-sided tender. Built in July 1925, No 4089 was withdrawn in September 1964 having amassed some 1,876,807 miles in service. *GWT/CGS*

Left:
The 'King' 4-6-0s were designed by Collett and constructed at Swindon between 1927 and 1930, and at that time were the most powerful engines in the country. The large, standard No 12 boiler helped to produce a tractive effort of over 40,000lb enabling the class to work the heaviest passenger services. The performance of the class was further improved when, between 1955 and 1958, they were all fitted with double chimneys. Standing between duties at Old Oak Common on 26 April 1962 is No 6019 *King Henry V*, carrying the 'Cambrian Coast Express' headboard, its next turn of duty. Built in July 1928, No 6019 received its double chimney in April 1957, and was finally withdrawn from service in September 1962. What is so sad is that many of the 'Kings' were in perfect working order when they were withdrawn. *GWT/CGS*

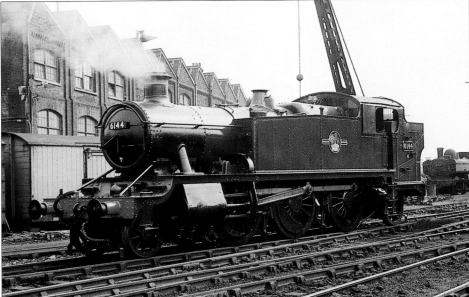

Centre left:
The mainstay of Western Region's London suburban service prior to the introduction of DMUs were the 70 Collett '6100' class 2-6-2Ts. They were built at Swindon between 1931 and 1935, especially to work the newly accelerated Great Western London suburban services. The class proved ideal for this type of work, with good acceleration and an excellent turn of speed. They operated these services for over 30 years, but the introduction of DMUs during 1960 saw many withdrawals. The surviving members of the class were demoted to goods services, and a number were still active in the Thames Valley right up until the end of steam in 1965. After Nationalisation the class was turned out in lined black, but from 1956 many were painted in lined-green livery. From the early 1960s, some non-main-line engines were turned out in green, but without lining. One of these was 2-6-2T No 6144 seen here at Swindon in ex-works condition on 9 April 1961. It carries an 84G Shrewsbury shedplate. Built at Swindon in November 1932, this large Prairie tank was withdrawn from service in June 1964. *GWT/CGS*

Lower left:
A great regret for Great Western enthusiasts was the withdrawal of the '4700' class 2-8-0s. These magnificent engines were built for use on the overnight fully fitted express freight services that were operated by the GWR, and later the Western Region. Designed by G. J. Churchward, the nine members of the class were built at Swindon between 1919 and 1923. The '4700s' could well be described as mixed traffic engines as, apart from their freight duties, for many years they saw regular use on 'extra' summer passenger services from Paddington to the South West. From new, they were turned out in black livery, but from 1957 they were painted in lined green, as can be seen on No 4706 at Southall shed yard on 17 April 1963. This locomotive was withdrawn from Southall in February 1964. *GWT/CGS*

WESTERN REGION STEAM

Above:

Many of the valley services in South Wales were operated by the '5600' class 0-6-2Ts. Introduced by the Great Western in 1924, they replaced older engines that had been inherited from South Wales railways at the 1923 Grouping. Altogether, 150 were built at Swindon, with a further 50 by Armstrong Whitworth. They were used on both passenger and goods services. The introduction of DMUs on valley services saw many of the class rendered redundant, but a number remained in use until the end of steam. This excellent view shows

No 6643 hauling the 'Rambling 56' special across Walnut Tree Viaduct on the Penrhos branch on 31 July 1965. The four-coach train comprised two BR Mk1s, an ex-GWR Hawksworth and a green-liveried ex-Southern Railway Bulleid-designed vehicle. The special train traversed a number of valley lines to commemorate the end of the '5600s' in South Wales. No 6643 was built at Swindon in September 1928, and was withdrawn from service just a few days after this run, in August 1965. Some nine members of the class have been preserved. *GWT/CGS*

Right:

Built for heavy goods work, the '7200' class 2-8-2Ts were introduced between 1934 and 1939 and were essentially rebuilds of older '4200' class 2-8-0Ts. By using the '4200' boilers and extending the frames a larger bunker could be fitted, thereby increasing coal capacity and giving a greater operating range. This then saw the '7200s' replacing the 'Aberdare' class 2-6-0s on medium- and long-distance coal trains. All 53 engines lasted well into Western Region days, the last examples not being withdrawn until June 1965. They were big and powerful engines, and their large bunkers had the same coal capacity as many tenders. From new, the '7200s' were painted in unlined black, a livery they carried all their working lives. No 7217, seen standing outside the shed at Gloucester on 13 April 1962, was rebuilt at Swindon in September 1934 using the boiler and frames from 2-8-0T No 5292 (built October 1930). It was withdrawn in July 1964. *GWT/CGS*

Above:

A true mixed traffic engine, the little '4300' class 2-6-0s were to be found on almost all types of working on the Great Western and Western Region system. Designed by Churchward, some 342 examples were built between 1911 and 1932. BR Western Region inherited 241 members of the class, and although a number were withdrawn during the 1950s, many lasted until 1964. No 7304 is seen here at Dulverton with a Taunton to Barnstaple service on 15 November 1962. It is fitted with original open-type cab and has outside steam pipes. Notice also the canvas cab extension, and single-line tablet exchange apparatus on the side of the tender. These engines were for many years the mainstay motive power on the Taunton to Barnstaple line, until replaced by DMUs in the early 1960s. Not all were built at Swindon, No 7304 being one of 35 examples constructed in 1921–2 by Robert Stephenson & Co. It was withdrawn in December 1963. *GWT/CGS*

Left:

Between 1936 and 1939, Collett introduced a new type of mixed traffic engine. The 'Grange' class was built using some parts from '4300' 2-6-0s, a class they were intended to replace. However, only 70 'Granges' were built. An easy running engine, the class soon proved to be very popular with drivers and firemen alike. The standard livery after Nationalisation was BR lined black, but from 1956 lined BR Brunswick green became the norm. This livery is seen here on No 6863 *Dolhywel Grange* as it stands in the yard at Plymouth Laira on 29 April 1962. The red D on the cab is the engine route classification, while the X denotes an engine capable of taking a heavier load than normal. No 6863 was built at Swindon in February 1939 and was withdrawn in November 1964, although a number were still in use right until the end of Western Region steam traction in December 1965. Unfortunately, none survived into preservation, but a replica is currently under construction. *GWT/CGS*

Right:
Lechlade, Gloucestershire, was situated just over the Oxfordshire border on the branch from Oxford to Fairford. On a sunny 14 May 1962 ex-Great Western '7400' class 0-6-0PT No 7404 of Oxford (81F) waits with the 12.44pm service from Oxford to Fairford. The fireman is filling his teapot with boiling water from the boiler. The small signalbox at Lechlade was situated on the platform and can be seen on the right. Passenger services between Oxford and Fairford were withdrawn on 18 June 1962.

The '7400s' were not auto-fitted and were designed for branch passenger and freight services. This was yet another ex-Great Western design of which further examples were built after Nationalisation. The first 30 were constructed in 1936–7, with a further batch of 20 in 1948–50. No 7404 was completed at Swindon during August 1936, and was withdrawn in June 1964. *GWT/CGS*

Above:
The 'Manor' class 4-6-0s were essentially a lighter version of the 'Grange' class. The first 20 were built at Swindon during 1938/39, primarily to replace some of the older members of the '4300' class 2-6-0s. They were initially put to use on some of the minor routes such as the Cheltenham to Banbury line, but were later to be found in Devon and on the Cambrian and West Wales lines. They were obviously successful as a further batch of 10 was constructed by

British Railways at Swindon in 1950. Pictured here at Carmarthen on 12 June 1963 with the up 'Pembroke Coast Express' is No 7814 *Fringford Manor*. Built in 1939, it has the standard Collett-design 3,000-gallon tender, as fitted to all members of the class. The BR livery was lined black, but from 1956 the 'Manors' were painted in lined green. Most of the class survived until 1964/5, and although *Fringford Manor* was withdrawn in November 1965 and broken up, no fewer than nine examples have been preserved. *GWT/CGS*

Left:
Ex-Great Western '8100' class 2-6-2T No 8104 passes the signalbox at Pershore on 22 June 1963 with a down freight. The '8100s' were essentially rebuilds, using the frames from older '5101' class 2-6-2Ts, but fitted with new, higher pressure boilers and smaller diameter wheels for better acceleration on suburban services. They were similar to the '6100' class 2-6-2Ts. No 8104 was built at Swindon in January 1939 using the frames from No 5124, and was withdrawn from service in December 1964. Pershore signalbox was constructed of timber with a slate roof and was opened on 22 April 1936. Containing a 44-lever frame, it closed on 18 September 1968. *GWT/PAF*

Above:
The largest class of steam locomotives, number-wise, on the Western Region was the '5700' 0-6-0PTs. No fewer than 863 examples were built between 1929 and 1950 and all passed into Western Region use. The class was used extensively over the whole system, and could be seen on branch passenger and goods services and general shunting duties. Pictured here arriving at Shepton Mallet High Street on 24 February 1962 with the 3.17pm service from Frome to Yatton is No 9628. It is in unlined black with early type BR lion and wheel emblem. Built at Swindon in 1943, No 9628 was withdrawn in March 1963. The Witham to Yatton branch was opened by the East Somerset Railway on 9 November 1858, and closed to passenger traffic on 9 September 1963. *GWT/PAF*

Right:
During 1933, the Great Western built 10 '9701' class condensing 0-6-0PTs, Nos 9701-9710, to replace the old 2-4-0T Metro Tanks on Metropolitan line workings to and from Smithfield Meat Market. (No 8700 was later modified and brought into line and numbered 9700.) These were a development of the '5700s', and apart from the condensing gear the engines were fitted with larger water tanks, a modified cab with sliding shutters, and ATC apparatus that was automatically clipped up when working over the electrified lines. The larger tank and cab can be seen clearly in this picture of No 9710 on general shunting duties at West Ealing on 27 April 1963. It is in unlined black livery with later type BR emblem. Built at Swindon in December 1933, No 9710 was withdrawn from Old Oak Common in October 1964. *GWT/CGS*

Below:
During 1952/3, BR Western Region constructed 25 LMS-type Ivatt-designed Class 2MT 2-6-0s at Swindon, ostensibly to replace the rather ancient Dean Goods and Cambrian 0-6-0s on Cambrian and Mid-Wales services. As a result of extensive testing at Swindon with Ivatt 2MT No 46413, the Swindon-built engines were fitted with a new design of blastpipe and chimney which improved their performance. Seen here at Brecon, after arrival with a passenger service from Moat Lane on 26 November 1962, is No 46511. Built at Swindon in 1952, it is in lined-black livery, but during the late1950s some of the WR members of the class were painted in BR lined green. The service from Brecon to Moat Lane was withdrawn on 31 December 1962. *GWT/CGS*

MAIN-LINE PASSENGER SERVICES

Left:
From 1927 until the early 1960s, the 'King' class 4-6-0s reigned supreme hauling the heaviest of the Great Western and Western Region passenger trains. The introduction of the 'Warship' class diesel-hydraulics during 1959 saw the 'Kings' relegated from the West of England services. However, they continued in use on trains to Cardiff and Wolverhampton. The disruption caused by the electrification of the Euston-Birmingham line in 1960 resulted in almost the whole class being used on the newly introduced one-hour interval service between Paddington and Wolverhampton.

Pictured here at Paddington on 7 May 1962, on train M20, the 4.10pm service to Wolverhampton, is No 6027 *King Richard I*. It is fitted with a double chimney and is resplendent in BR lined-green livery. The 'Kings' were displaced by the 'Western'

Class 52s on the Wolverhampton services with the introduction of the Winter 1962 timetable and, in one stroke, the remaining members of the class were withdrawn from service. Built at Swindon in July 1930, No 6027 was withdrawn from traffic in September 1962. *GWT/CGS Below:*

Right:
In 1956, the Western Region management decided to resurrect some of the named express services from the past, with a number of new additions to the list. Instructions were given that engines would be clean and carry the new 'named-train' headboards.
To complement the new services several rakes of BR Mk1 coaches were painted in chocolate and cream livery to reflect the old company. This *Famous Named Trains* pamphlet was issued by the Western Region publicity department in 1959.
Author's collection

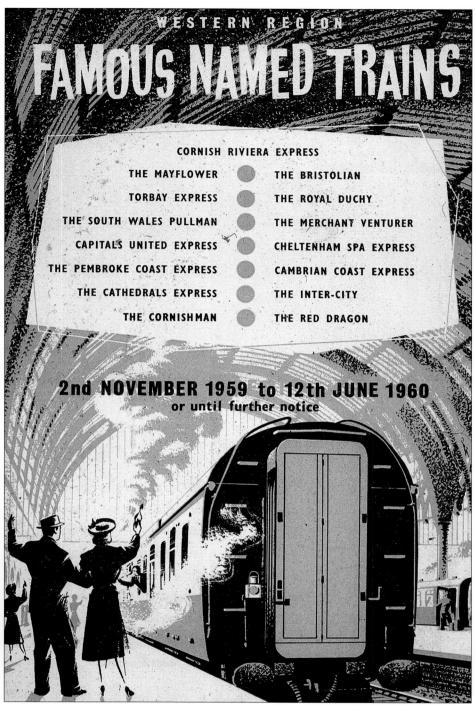

Left;
Probably the Great Western's most famous service, after the 'Cornish Riviera Express' was the pre-war 'Cheltenham Flyer', which was advertised as 'The Fastest Train in the World'. This service had been withdrawn during World War 2 and was not really resurrected afterwards.

The 'Cheltenham Spa Express', the 8am service from Cheltenham Spa St James to Paddington and the 4.55pm return, was one of the new named-train services introduced in 1956. Although not quite as fast as the old 'Flyer' it was still 'Castle'-hauled and is seen here at West Ealing on its approach to London on 19 March 1962 behind No 7034 *Ince Castle*. This was one of the very last batch of 'Castles' to be built by BR at Swindon. It entered service in August 1950 and was fitted with a double chimney in December 1959; it was withdrawn from service in June 1965. *CGS/Colour-Rail/BRW1873Right:*

Above:
Another new named train was introduced in 1957, the 'Cathedrals Express' — the 7.45am up Hereford, Oxford and Paddington service, the down service returning at 4.45pm. Again, a complete set of chocolate and cream Mk1s was provided by the Western Region. The 1957 loading was 10 coaches, but by 1959 this had been reduced to eight. The up service is seen here at Didcot East curve on 27 March 1963, hauled by spotless Worcester-based 'Castle' No 7027 *Thornbury Castle*. The illusion is somewhat destroyed by the route code A22 chalked on the smokebox door. This locomotive was built by BR at Swindon in August 1949 and was withdrawn from service in December 1963. After spending many years in Woodhams' scrapyard, and then stored at Tyseley, it has been moved to the Railway Age, Crewe. *GWT/CGS*

ABOVE:
'King' class 4-6-0 No 6028 *King George VI* powers the up 'Red Dragon', the 7.30am service from Carmarthen to Paddington, through Ealing Broadway on 17 March 1962. Apart from a maroon restaurant car, the train comprises almost a full set of BR Mk1s in chocolate and cream, fitted with the new B4 bogies. The 'Kings' took over from the BR 'Britannia' 4-6-2s on these services during 1959/60. No 6028 was built in July 1930 as *King Henry II*, but was renamed in January 1937. Fitted with a double chimney in January 1957, it was withdrawn from service in November 1962. *GWT/CGS*

Above:

To commemorate the withdrawal of the 'King' class from passenger services, the Stephenson Locomotive Society ran a farewell railtour on 28 April 1963 from Birmingham Snow Hill to Southall, Swindon and then back to Birmingham. The special was hauled by No 6018 *King Henry VI*, seen here passing through Shrivenham on its way to Swindon. The smokebox number and shedplate have been removed and the number painted in GW style on the front bufferbeam. No 6018 had actually been withdrawn from service in December 1962, but was reinstated for the railtour, after which it was placed into store at Swindon for a few more months before being cut up. The station at Shrivenham was closed to passengers on 7 December 1964. *GWT/PAF*

Right:

Another sad occasion took place on 11 June 1965 when 'Castle' No 7029 *Clun Castle* hauled the last scheduled steam service out of Paddington, the 16.18 service to Banbury. No 7029 is seen here passing North Acton en route to Banbury. The engine carries the Great Western coat of arms but still retains its smokebox numberplate, under the route identification number. The engine number has also been painted on the front bufferbeam, which is technically incorrect as the engine was built by BR at Swindon in May 1950 and was fitted with a smokebox numberplate from new. No 7029 was fitted with a double chimney in October 1959 and was withdrawn from service in December 1965. Sold privately, and kept in working order by the late P. B. Whitehouse, *Clun Castle* is now preserved at Tyseley. *GWT/CGS*

BR STANDARDS

Between 1951 and 1960, the British Railways Board constructed 12 new classes of BR Standard steam locomotives comprising a total of 999 locomotives. The design team was headed by R. A. Riddles, with individual class designs being undertaken at the Swindon, Derby, Doncaster and Brighton drawing offices. Swindon was responsible for the design and construction of the Class 3 2-6-0 77000s and the Class 3 2-6-4T 82000s. The 4-6-0 Class 4 75000s were designed at Derby and built at Swindon, as were 54 of the Brighton-designed '9F' class 2-10-0s. However, only a small percentage of the Swindon-built locomotives were actually allocated to the Western Region. The new engines supposedly incorporated the best design features from each of the 'Big Four' railway companies, but in reality were based mainly on LMS designs.

Above:
Only a small number of the BR Standard Class 5 4-6-0s were allocated to the Western Region. Here they were used on both passenger and goods services.
No 73012 was built at Derby in 1951, and is seen in BR lined-green livery at its home shed, Swindon (82C) on 7 August 1962.

The Swindon engines were generally used on fast fitted freights. Other members of the class were allocated to Shrewsbury, where they were used mainly for services over the Central Wales line to Swansea. Those at Bath Green Park saw use on Somerset & Dorset services. *GWT/CGS*

Above:
In 1952, a number of the new BR 'Britannia' Class 7MT 4-6-2s were allocated to the Western Region. These were the first Pacifics to run regularly over GWR metals since the withdrawal of Churchward's *Great Bear* 4-6-2 in 1924. Initially, the 'Britannias' were placed on services in the South West of England, but were not popular with the locomotive crews. They eventually ended up at Cardiff Canton where they were used on express services to and from South Wales, including the 'Capitals United' and 'Red Dragon' services. All 15 of the Western Region Pacifics were named after earlier Great Western engines.

Passing Reading West Junction is Cardiff Canton-allocated No 70024 *Vulcan* with the 1.55pm service from Paddington to Pembroke Dock. The engine is still fitted with the early type handrails on the smoke deflectors but these were gradually removed from Western Region 'Britannias' and replaced with recessed handholds, after a crash involving No 70026 *Polar Star* at Milton in 1955. In the subsequent enquiry the early-type handrails were blamed for partially obscuring visibility from the footplate. As with other Standard classes, the engine was designed with a high running plate to facilitate easy maintenance. The introduction of the new 'Warship' diesels on services to the South West released a number of 'Kings', which were then used on services to South Wales. The 'Britannias' became surplus to requirements and were transferred to the London Midland Region during 1959–60. *Colour-Rail/BRW1138*

Above:

A total of 80 BR Standard Class 4 4-6-0s were built at Swindon between 1951 and 1956. No 75071 was one of the final batch to be built in 1956, and is seen entering Radstock North on 12 October 1963 with the 3.30pm service from Bath to Templecombe. The engine is painted in BR lined-black livery. Under the regional boundary changes the whole of the Somerset & Dorset line was placed under Western Region control from 1 January 1963, although the region had been responsible for the section between Bath and Templecombe from 1958. In the background is the small stone-built two-road engine shed at Radstock North, a sub shed of Bath (82F). The Somerset & Dorset line, together with Radstock shed, was closed on 7 March 1966. *GWT/MY*

Right:

Although designed at Derby in 1953, the 78000-series 2-6-0s were all built at Darlington and were a direct copy of Ivatt's 1946 designed LMS Class 2, 2-6-0s, but incorporating the benefit of Swindon's draughting improvements. The first 10 were allocated to the Western Region for use on Cambrian and Mid-Wales services, and by the mid-1950s examples were working from Machynlleth, Worcester, Hereford and Gloucester. No 78004 is seen here at Gloucester Horton Road on 13 April 1962, in lined-green livery and carrying an 85B Gloucester shedplate. Most of the Western Region engines were reallocated to the London Midland Region during the 1960s. No 78004 was withdrawn from service in 1964, but two other members of the class, Nos 78001 and 78006, remained at Gloucester until the end of WR steam in December 1965. *GWT/CGS*

Above:

As already mentioned, the 82000-series Class 3 2-6-4Ts were designed and built at Swindon. First introduced in 1952, the class eventually numbered 45 locomotives, which were allocated to the Western, Southern and North Eastern Regions. The Western Region examples generally worked branch-line services in the South Wales and Bristol areas. However, some also saw service on the Somerset & Dorset line, both before and after its takeover by the region on 1 January 1963. Standing on the turntable at Bath Green Park on 5 September 1962 is No 82004. All of the class were turned out from new in lined-black livery, but from 1956 a number of the Western Region examples were painted in unlined green, as seen here. *GWT/CGS*

Left:

The BR Standard Class 9F 2-10-0s were introduced by BR in 1954 with the first eight allocated from new to 86A Newport Ebbw Junction. By the early 1960s, further examples were operating from Old Oak Common, Southall, Oxford, Cardiff and Banbury. The class was used on heavy freight and mineral services throughout the Western Region.

Apart from No 92220 *Evening Star*, all the other members of the class were painted in unlined black, as seen in this picture of No 92240 standing in the shed yard at Oxford on 28 March 1963. It is fitted with a double chimney and carries an 81C Southall shedplate. Built by BR at Crewe in 1958, it was withdrawn from Southall in September 1965 and ended up at Woodhams' scrapyard at Barry. It was purchased for preservation in October 1978 and taken to the Bluebell Railway where it underwent extensive restoration before being returned to traffic in 1990. *GWT/CGS*

NARROW GAUGE

Right:
For a number of years the Western Region operated two narrow gauge lines, both situated in Mid Wales. The 2ft 6in gauge Welshpool & Llanfair Light Railway was opened between Welshpool and Llanfair Caereinion on 4 April 1903 and was worked by the Cambrian Railways company. It had two small 0-6-0 tank engines, No 1 *The Earl* and No 2 *The Countess*, both built by Beyer Peacock & Co in September 1902. In 1922, the Great Western renumbered them 822 and 823 respectively. The new numberplates were positioned in the centre of the water tanks and the nameplates were moved to the cabside. Interestingly, the name on No 823 was shortened to *Countess* in order to fit it under the cab. Passenger services over the line were withdrawn in February 1931, but it continued in use for goods traffic until closure in November 1956. The two engines were then placed in store at Oswestry where they remained until sold to the Welshpool & Llanfair Railway Preservation Society. No 822 was purchased in 1961 and No 823 in 1962.

This delightful view shows No 822 emerging from the gap between the houses as it crosses Church Street, Welshpool, with a short goods service, in September 1956. The engine is in plain black livery and unnamed, the nameplates on both locomotives having been removed for safe keeping. *JE/Colour-Rail/BRW324*

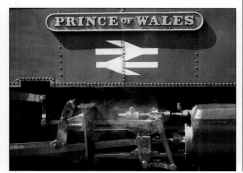

Above left:
On 1 January 1963, the Vale of Rheidol operation was transferred to the London Midland Region which initially retained the Western Region green livery. However, in around 1968, corporate identity went mad as the two operational locomotives were painted in BR standard blue livery, and adorned with a large BR double-arrow logo. The effect was a bit overpowering on such a small locomotive, as seen on this side view of No 9 *Prince of Wales* taken on 25 June 1974. The line remained part of the BR network until 1988 when, on 4 November, No 7 *Owain Glyndwr* had the honour of working the very last BR steam-hauled passenger service, after which, and apart from a couple of specials, the line was closed, even though it had been a successful tourist line for BR. The whole operation was then sold to the Brecon Mountain Railway Co Ltd on 31 March 1989. *GWT/MY*

Above right:
After the withdrawal of main-line steam traction in August 1968, the only steam services operated by British Rail were those on the Vale of Rheidol Railway. This 1ft 11½in gauge line was opened for passengers on 22 December 1902, and was absorbed by the Cambrian Railways Co on 1 July 1913. The Cambrian itself was absorbed by the Great Western in 1922. The VofRR was under the control of the Western Region after Nationalisation. Locomotives Nos 7 and 8 were built at Swindon in 1923. In 1924 another new locomotive was built, although it was officially known as a rebuild of No 1213, taking its number until 1949 when it became No 9. All three have survived and in June 1956 they were named: No 7 *Owain Glyndwr*, No 8 *Llewelyn* and No 9 *Prince of Wales*. Pictured here is No 8 *Llewelyn* as it approaches Capel Bangor on 22 August 1966 with the 1.30pm service from Devils Bridge to Aberystwyth. The engine is in BR green with the later type BR crest. *GWT/PAF*

SWINDON WORKS

The Great Western works at Swindon was established in 1843 by Daniel (later Sir Daniel) Gooch. Originally opened for locomotive maintenance and construction, the works were extended during the 1850s when the carriage shops were transferred from Paddington. At this time the works covered an area of about 14 acres, but further expansion continued and during 1900 a new, larger locomotive erecting shop ('A' Shop) was opened. This already large building was extended again during 1921. 'A' Shop alone covered an area of some 11½ acres. The importance of the GWR to the town is illustrated by the work it provided for the inhabitants. In 1901, the population of Swindon numbered around 45,000 of whom 12,000 were employed in the works. By the 1930s, expansion had reached its peak, the works covering an area of 323 acres, of which 73 acres were under cover. The complete withdrawal of WR steam in 1965 saw the works rationalised with the closure of the carriage shops and other steam-related buildings. Diesel production at Swindon for BR came to an end in October 1965 with the completion of 650hp 0-6-0DH No D9555. Diesel locomotive and multiple-unit repairs continued until the complete closure of the works in 1986. Today, much of the area is covered with housing, although some of the old engineering shops are now in use as a retail outlet, and 'Steam', the Museum of the Great Western Railway. The works drawing office forms part of the National Historic Monuments HQ.

Above:
It is difficult to illustrate the immense size of 'A' Shop. This picture shows one small area, and was taken on 24 March 1963. Locomotives seen under repair are, from right to left: '5700' class 0-6-0PT No 9680, '2884' class 2-8-0 No 3866, and 'Castle' class 4-6-0 No 7025 *Sudeley Castle*. In the foreground are the tracks of the large traverser used for moving locomotives in and out of the shop. Situated overhead were a number of movable heavy lifting cranes. *GWT/CGS*

Above right:
A typical Swindon Works scene shows an ex-works engine outside 'A' Shop and awaiting test, on 24 March 1963. Former GWR '8100' class 2-6-2T No 8109 looks superb in unlined black. The main door to 'A' Shop can be seen on the left. The '8100s' were rebuilds using the frames from some of the older '5101' class 2-6-2Ts.

No 8109 was built in November 1939 using the frames from No 5115, which itself had been rebuilt at Swindon in May 1928, and it spent most of its life working in the Birmingham area. It was withdrawn in June 1965. *GWT/CGS*

Below right:
'Castle' class 4-6-0 No 7007 *Ogmore Castle*, which was completed in July 1946, was the last express passenger engine to be built by the Great Western at Swindon. In January 1948, and in commemoration of the demise of the old company, it was renamed *Great Western*. The nameplate is pictured here, on 28 October 1962. Notice also the Great Western coat of arms on the splasher. 'Castle' class engines, other than those named after Earls, had the small brass 'Castle Class' plate fitted under the name. No 7007 was withdrawn from service in February 1963. GWT/CGS

Above:
In later years, the old six-road carriage 'stock' shed at Swindon was used for storing locomotives. It was here in the late 1950s that 'Star' class 4-6-0 No 4003 *Lode Star*, and Dean Goods No 2516 were kept. Seen here in store on 7 August 1962 is restored ex-GW diesel railcar No 4. Built by AEC at Southall in September 1934, it was withdrawn from service in July 1958. Together with the two steam locomotives it was later placed on display in the Great Western Railway Museum, a converted chapel on the Bath Road in Swindon, which was opened on 23 June 1962. This museum closed in 2001, and the stock, with the exception of No 4003 which is currently at the National Railway Museum, York, moved to the new and larger 'Steam' museum that has been established in part of the old works. GWT/CGS

Left:
The rapid withdrawal of steam during the 1960s resulted in large numbers of redundant locomotives being stored at Swindon prior to being cut up. Standing in the yard outside 'A' Shop on 7 October 1962 are 'King' class 4-6-0s Nos 6024 *King Edward I* and 6023 *King Edward II*, together with 'Castle' class 4-6-0 No 4086 *Builth Castle*. All three were sold to scrap merchants for cutting up. The 'Castle' was cut up at Cashmores at Newport, but the two 'Kings' ended up at Woodhams' yard at Barry, and have since been preserved. No 6024 arrived at the Buckinghamshire Railway Centre from Barry in March 1973, and since completion of restoration in 1989 has made many main-line runs. No 6023 was moved to Bristol in December 1984, and to Didcot Railway Centre in March 1990 where it is currently being restored. *GWT/PAF*

Above:

The last steam engine to be built at Swindon Works was BR Standard '9F' No 92220. Constructed in January 1960, the engine was initially turned out in black livery, but because it was also the last steam locomotive to be built for BR, the Western Region held a competition to find a suitable name for the engine. The winning entry was *Evening Star*, a name originally carried by Great Western 'Star' class 4-6-0 No 4002, which had been built at Swindon in 1907 and withdrawn in 1933. For the naming ceremony, which took place at Swindon Works

on 18 March 1960, the engine was repainted in fully lined BR Brunswick green and fitted with a copper capped chimney and brass nameplates.

This engine, like many other '9Fs', saw use on both freight and passenger traffic. In 1962, it was allocated to Bath Green Park, for working passenger services over the old Somerset & Dorset route to Bournemouth. It is pictured here at Bath Green Park MPD on 5 September 1962. It was subsequently preserved as part of the National Collection. *GWT/CGS*

Right:
The nameplate and commemorative plaque carried by No 92220, taken on the same day.
GWT/CGS

Above:
In later years the works' yards at Swindon became a store for withdrawn diesels. Inside 'A' Shop, Class 08 diesel shunters were both repaired and dismantled. In this picture, taken in April 1984, No 08617 is being cut up. Built at Derby in September 1959 as No D3784, it was withdrawn from service and placed into store in October 1981. On the left and under repair is Western Region PW Department 0-6-0DE shunter No 97653. Built by Ruston & Hornsby in August 1959 as No PWM653 it was based at Reading for a number of years, but withdrawn from Cardiff in August 1992 and partially dismantled, the remains now being in the hands of a locomotive dealer. *Author*

Left:
As well as locomotives, the Great Western also established its carriage works at Swindon, and over the years thousands of carriages and wagons were built there. Withdrawn from service and standing outside the stock shed at Swindon on 20 September 1964 is ex-GWR 'County' class 4-6-0 No 1010 *County of Caernarvon* and ex-GWR Dynamometer Car No W7W. The Great Western was the first British railway company to carry out controlled road testing of locomotives. The Dynamometer Car was designed by Churchward and built at Swindon in 1901 under wagon Lot No 293. Numbered 790 by the GWR, it was renumbered by the Western Region in 1948, and after many years of service was withdrawn in 1961. The car, which was 45ft long, was fitted with a clerestory roof, observation ends and side lookouts; notice also, the retractable flangeless wheel for speed recording purposes. *GWT/PAF*

Above:

The 1901 Churchward test vehicle was replaced by a new Dynamometer Car, No DW150192, seen here at Oxford on 28 March 1963. Built as Hawksworth all-Third passenger coach No 7969 (Diagram C82) at Swindon in August 1946, it was converted for diesel locomotive testing by the Western Region in May 1961. A number of the instruments from No W7W were reused in the later vehicle. In 1967, the Dynamometer Car moved from Swindon to the Research Centre at Derby, and in 1983, it was sold to the *Duke of Gloucester* preservation group for use as a support coach. *GWT/CGS*

Right:

Another ex-Great Western coach that saw further use on the Western Region was No KDW150266. Built at Swindon in 1925 to Diagram H33 Lot 1349, it started life as bow-ended Composite/Restaurant Car No 9580. The coach was converted into an Inspection Saloon for the Signal & Telegraph Department in 1960, fitted with end windows and renumbered KDW150266. It is seen here, in chocolate and cream livery with full yellow ends, standing outside the closed Reading station East Main signalbox, in March 1984. After withdrawal, it was preserved on the East Lancashire Railway. *Author*

STATIONS

The Western Region inherited hundreds of stations from the Great Western, ranging from the superb stations at Paddington and Bristol Temple Meads right down to the humble single-platform halt. The examples selected illustrate a variety of styles.

Above:
Birmingham Snow Hill was one of the largest stations on the Western Region. Its 12 platforms were located below road level, trains entering from the south via the 564yd Snow Hill Tunnel, and from the north by the 132yd Hockley Tunnel. The fine frontage and entrance to the station are seen here on 20 November 1966. Built by the GWR in 1863 as a 126-room hotel, due to a lack of patronage it was closed in 1909. The building was subsequently converted into offices for goods and station administration, although a public restaurant was retained on the ground floor. The rundown of passenger services saw the partial closure of Snow Hill in 1968; the entrance building subsequently fell out of use, and was demolished in 1969. The station itself was closed on 6 March 1972. The entrance to the station can be seen in the centre of the picture. The revival of the railway in the Birmingham area under the banner of the West Midlands PTE saw a new station opened at Snow Hill on 2 October 1987. *GWT/CGS*

Above right:
The station building and ground frame hut at Hemyock are seen here on 15 November 1962. Hemyock was the terminus of the branch from Tiverton Junction and was a typical Great Western country terminus station. The small brick entrance structure dates from the opening of the branch in 1893. Standing on the platform outside the seven-lever ground frame hut are seven fire buckets. The wooden station nameboard is mounted on sections of redundant rail.

Passenger services were withdrawn on 9 September 1963, and the ground frame taken out of use on the same day. The large building in the background is the St Ivel Creamery which continued to be served by rail until the branch was closed to freight traffic on 31 October 1975. *GWT/CGS*

Lower right:
A station had been opened by the Great Western at Castle Hill, Ealing, on 1 March 1871. This was renamed West Ealing on 1 July 1899. The building, seen here on 9 December 1962, was built using light brick and probably dates from the rebuilding of the road overbridge by the Great Western during 1908. A standard-type brown and cream enamel station nameboard has been fixed to what appears to be a later addition to the roof. *GWT/CGS*

Above:

These advertising hoardings greeted travellers at Marlow, Buckinghamshire, in the 1960s. The 'Great Marlow Railway' branch from Marlow Road (Bourne End) was opened on 28 June 1873. The brick station with its arched windows and ornate chimneys, and the goods shed beyond, date from the opening of the branch and can be seen in this picture taken on 20 March 1962. The smaller brick office on the end appears to be a later extension. Rationalisation of the Marlow branch saw the station closed on 10 July 1967 and the services switched to a new platform which had been erected in the old goods yard. The old building was soon demolished, and the site is now covered with industrial buildings. *GWT/CGS*

Below:

The Abingdon Railway Company opened its branch from Abingdon Junction, on the Oxford line, to Abingdon on 2 June 1856. The line was extended to a new station at Radley on 8 September 1873. The main station building at Abingdon was rebuilt after an accident on 22 April 1908, which demolished the original structure. Waiting at the single platform on 19 May 1962 is Pressed Steel Motor Brake Second No W55031 on the 9.50am service to Radley. DMUs had taken over from steam during the autumn of 1961. Abingdon was closed to passengers on 9 September 1963, and to freight in 1980 with the closure of the MG car plant. The loading bay for new cars is on the left. The branch then became what was essentially a long siding serving a coal yard, until it was finally closed in 1984. *GWT/PAF*

Right:
Dartmouth, Devon, was a station without any trains. The 3¾-mile branch from Brixham Road (later Churston) to Kingswear was opened by the South Devon Railway on 16 August 1864. The opening also included a ferry service from the railhead at Kingswear across the River Dart to the village of Dartmouth and the nearby Royal Naval College. Rail tickets from Dartmouth were issued to all parts of the country, but booking facilities were withdrawn by the Western Region in 1964. Passenger services were withdrawn between Paignton and Kingswear by the Western Region in 1972 but the branch has since reopened, and is now operated as the Paignton & Dartmouth Railway. The large 'station' building at Dartmouth is pictured here, on 20 September 1966. Constructed of wood with a slate roof, inside was a large waiting area, toilets and ticket office; it is now in use as a cafe and tourist centre.
GWT/PAF

Above:
Shepherds, pictured here on 17 June 1962, was a typical Great Western country station and was situated on the single-line branch from Truro to Newquay. The 8.45am service from Truro to Newquay, which has just arrived, appears to be formed of three single-car Class 121/122 units and a trailer car. The loop platform at Shepherds was constructed of wood with a small brick waiting room. The main station entrance and ticket office are on the left, with a small awning which offered some protection in bad weather. The station was opened on 2 January 1905, but was closed when passenger services were withdrawn from the Newquay, Perranporth and Chacewater branch on 4 February 1963.
GWT/CGS

Left:

The Great Western provided halt platforms on many of its lines. The halt was the smallest and cheapest station to construct. A typical halt comprised just one or two, usually wooden, platforms, a corrugated iron shelter, and sometimes lights. To save money there were no ticketing facilities or staff.

Cashes Green Halt, Stroud, was a typical Great Western halt, its two wooden platforms serving both up and down lines. It is pictured here on 3 October 1964 with a Chalford to Gloucester service hauled by '9400' class 0-6-0PT No 8402. The corrugated iron waiting shelters have round roofs rather than being of the more usual pagoda type. Cashes Green Halt was opened on 22 January 1930, and cost just £185 to construct, due in part to the reuse of material from the closed Chalvey Halt on the Windsor branch. Cashes Green Halt was closed on 2 November 1964. *GWT/MY*

Above:

The branch from West Drayton to Staines was opened by the Great Western on 2 November 1885. The station building at Staines West is seen here on 4 January 1964. The building was originally a private dwelling house, but to reduce costs it was purchased by the GWR and converted into the branch terminus. The branch was closed to passenger traffic on 27 March 1965, and today the former terminus building is Grade 2 listed, and has in recent years been tastefully converted into luxury flats. *GWT/CGS*

Below:

The unusual terminus building at Cirencester Town on 28 March 1963. Standing at the platform is AC Cars railbus No W79978 with a service from Kemble. The Brunel-designed station building was constructed in Cotswold stone by the Cheltenham & Great Western Union Railway in around 1841. The awning and parcels entrance are later additions. The branch from Kemble was closed to passengers on 6 April 1964. The building still survives and is Grade 2 listed, while the station yard is used as a car park and bus station. No W79978 is preserved on the Colne Valley Railway. *GWT/CGS*

Left:

The Beeching cuts of the 1960s saw the closure of many lines and stations. This resulted in the loss of a number of early GW designs, one of which was the very attractive Pauling-designed train shed at Thame, pictured here on 28 March 1963, just two months after closure to passenger traffic. Notice the wooden construction which dates from the opening of the first section of the Princes Risborough to Oxford branch in August 1862. Also in view is the small goods shed, and on the right, Thame signalbox. Thame was closed to parcels and goods traffic on 10 October 1966, and it was around this time that the station building was demolished. The branch continued to be used as a diversionary route until the central section between Thame and Morris Cowley was closed to all traffic on 1 May 1967. The section from Thame to Princes Risborough remained open for oil traffic until it was closed in September 1991. Part of the route is now a cycle path. *GWT/CGS*

Above:
The first major station to be completely rebuilt by the Western Region under the 1955 Modernisation Plan was at Banbury. The old station was designed by Richard Pauling with an overall roof, and was similar in style to the station at Thame. Banbury was a much larger structure with an internal footbridge connecting the two main platforms and bays. By Nationalisation, the building was in a poor state, and during 1952 the overall roof was removed. Reconstruction work started in 1956 and was completed during 1958. The new, modern concrete and brick structure was entered via a large ticket hall, the new platforms and bays being reached via a large overbridge, which also contained a buffet bar.

The new station can be seen in the background as 'King' class 4-6-0 No 6016 *King Edward V* waits to depart with the 8.40am service from Birkenhead on 30 July 1962. It was during this period that the 'Kings' were operating a one-hour interval service between Paddington and Birmingham. Banbury station has in recent years received a facelift, but some of the bay platforms opened in 1958 are now unused. *GWT/CGS*

Left:
During the 1960s and '70s the Western Region undertook modernisation work at a number of stations. One of those was at Oxford where the old Great Western station dated from 1852, but over the years had seen many alterations, the last major one being in 1890 when the overall roof was removed. By the late 1960s the main buildings were in a poor state of repair, and in 1970 were demolished and replaced by a new station. The main upside entrance building is seen here on 26 May 1978. The whole structure was built 'on the cheap' with flat roofs that soon leaked, and by the 1980s the main buildings were probably in a worse condition than the ex-GWR station they had replaced. In 1990, the upside buildings seen here were demolished and replaced by a new, larger and more permanent structure which is still in use today. *GWT/MY*

EARLY DIESELS AND GAS TURBINES

The Great Western first introduced diesel railcars during the 1930s, which proved to be very successful, and continued to be operated by the Western Region until 1962. The Great Western was the first of the 'Big Four' companies to use this type of traction in regular passenger service. The first four railcars were built by AEC at Southall, and after a number of trial runs No 1 was put into revenue-earning service on 5 February 1934. Railcars Nos 5-18 were built by the Gloucester Railway Carriage & Wagon Co using AEC engines and became known as 'Flying Bananas' because of their shape. Three of the early railcars were fitted with toilets and buffet bars for use on express services between Cardiff and Birmingham, and later on services between Swansea and Cheltenham.

Below:
This photograph, taken in April 1958, shows railcar No W14W, in BR 'strawberry and cream' livery, on a local service at Birmingham Snow Hill. This was the basic streamlined design used on the first 18 railcars, No 14 being introduced on 23 March 1936, and giving excellent service until withdrawn in August 1960. *JE/Colour-Rail/DE483*

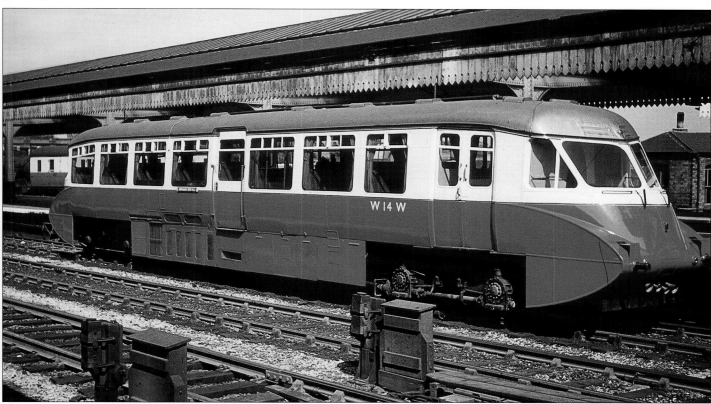

Right:
The success of the railcars prompted the Great Western to order a further batch of 20. These were built to a different design, to give more floor space. They were fitted with AEC engines, but with the bodies and chassis constructed at Swindon. All the new cars were fitted with standard draw gear, and as in the first batch, one was built specifically for parcels traffic, while another four were designed as two pairs of twin units to allow a standard passenger coach to be attached between the two.

Standing at Bewdley with the 1.12pm service to Highley on 21 July 1962 is railcar No W20W. Built at Swindon in June 1940, it is seen here in BR 'strawberry and cream' livery with white cab roofs. It was withdrawn in October 1962 and has since been preserved on the Kent & East Sussex Railway. *GWT/PAF*

Left:
Six of the later batch of railcars survived in service until October 1962, some of which were painted in the standard BR DMU green livery. This can be seen on No W26W as it stands outside Worcester locomotive works on 25 July 1962. No 26 was completed at Swindon on 18 September 1940, and withdrawn in October 1962. Three of the GWR diesel railcars, Nos 4, 20, and 22, have been preserved, the latter in working order at Didcot. *GWT/CGS*

Above:
As well as the railcars the Great Western also considered using diesel power for shunting, and to this end purchased a diesel-electric locomotive from R. & W. Hawthorn, Leslie & Co Ltd in April 1936. It was initially numbered 2 in Great Western stock, and saw much of its use in Acton yard. In February 1948, the 0-6-0DE was renumbered 15100 by British Railways, a number it retained until its withdrawal in April 1965. It is seen here at Southall on 10 December 1962, in green livery, but with the early type lion and wheel emblem. Note the large builder's plate under the number (Hawthorn, Leslie No 3853). Interestingly, it was the only Great Western locomotive to be renumbered under the BR renumbering scheme. Despite its success it was not until 1948/49 that a further seven similar shunters, Nos 15101-15107, were built at Swindon for use on the newly formed Western Region. *GWT/CGS*

Left:
After the relative success of the diesel railcars it is surprising that the Great Western declined to experiment further with diesel traction and, instead, ordered two experimental gas turbine locomotives. Although ordered by the GWR, both of these locomotives were delivered well after Nationalisation. The first of these was A1A-A1A No 18000, which was taken into stock on 9 May 1950, had been ordered in 1946, and is pictured here outside the stock shed at Swindon 9 March 1961 in green livery with red bufferbeams and side stripe. No 18000 was designed and built by Brown Boveri in Switzerland, but was never very reliable, although it did amass some 41,000 miles in service during 1951. It was used mainly on Paddington to Plymouth and Bristol services, but often spent long periods out of action in Swindon Works. The main problem with gas turbine locomotives was their poor fuel ecnomy. The author was hauled from Swindon to Didcot by this locomotive after a Sunday visit to Swindon Works in 1958. It was withdrawn from service in December 1960, and was returned to Switzerland for use as a mobile laboratory. After a number of years on display it was returned to the UK, minus its engine, and is currently on show at the Railway Age at Crewe. *GWT/CGS*

Above:
The second WR gas turbine locomotive was the Metropolitan-Vickers/Hawksworth-design Co-Co No 18100. This was delivered to Swindon on 16 December 1951 and entered service in May 1952, and just like fellow gas turbine No 18000, proved to be equally unreliable and uneconomic to run. It was withdrawn from service in January 1958, and converted by the builders into an experimental 25kV electric locomotive, No E2001, and used for crew training during the early days of the LMR electrification. It stood out of use for a number of years before being cut up in December 1972. This rare colour picture was taken in 1952 and shows No 18100 brand new at Metropolitan-Vickers' Trafford Park Works. It is in BR black livery with lion and wheel emblem. When running, which apparently was not very often, No 18100 was used on services between Paddington and Bristol. *KM/Colour-Rail/DE1452*

Above left:
Depicted here at Plymouth Laira on 29 April 1962 is the third 'Warship' to be delivered, No D602 *Bulldog*. It entered service in November 1958 and is seen in lined-green livery with half yellow ends. In 1962, the D600-series 'Warships' were restricted to working services between Plymouth and Penzance. As already mentioned, these early NBL 'Warships' were never very reliable, and all five were withdrawn from service in December 1967. Interestingly, No D601 *Ark Royal* languished at Woodhams' yard at Barry, pretty well intact, until June 1980. A preservation proposal received no support whatsoever. *CGS/Colour-Rail/DE2203*

Below left:
The first of the 'Warship' class Type 4s (Class 42) No D800 *Sir Brian Robertson*, was built at Swindon in July 1958, and was named at Paddington on 14 July 1958 by the chairman of the British Transport Commission, Sir Brian Robertson. The new 'Warships' were of a lighter design than the D600s and were fitted with two Maybach engines producing around 2,200bhp. The design was based on the German V200/0 diesel-hydraulics. No D800 is seen here at Old Oak Common on 5 August 1962 and is basically as built with train description discs, which were fitted to the first 13 members of the class only. The four-character headcode display panel is a later addition. No D800 is in plain green livery with a white side stripe and red-backed nameplate; notice also the red 83D (Plymouth) shedplate below the cab. Initially, these locomotives were introduced on services to Bristol and the South West and were allocated to the new diesel depot at Plymouth Laira. No D800 was withdrawn in October 1968. A total of 71 'Warships' were built: 38 at Swindon (Class 42) and a further 33 by the North British Locomotive Company (Class 43). *CGS/Colour-Rail/DE2205*

Below:
No D867 *Zenith* speeds through West Ealing with the down 'Cornish Riviera Express' on 16 March 1962. This was one of the last batch of Swindon-built Class 42 'Warships', being completed in April 1961. It is in plain green with four-character headcode panel, but no train description discs. The whole train comprises BR Mk1 coaches painted in chocolate and cream livery. No D867 was withdrawn from Plymouth Laira in October 1971. *GWT/CGS*

THE DIESEL-HYDRAULICS

Unlike the other regions which favoured the diesel-electric system, the Western Region decided to adopt diesel-hydraulic transmission for its locomotives, and just like Great Western days, retained the policy of naming its main-line engines.

The first such locomotive to be delivered to the region was 'Warship' class Type 4 A1A-A1A (later Class 41) No D600 *Active*. Built by the North British Locomotive Company, it was the first of five members of the class, and was handed over in January 1958. Unfortunately, and as a portent of things to come, it broke down on a demonstration run on 17 February 1958 when one of its two engines failed. The train had a number of VIPs on board, but was able to continue by running on its one remaining engine.

Above left:
Class 42 No D813 *Diadem*, built at Swindon in December 1959, speeds past Starcross on 20 September 1966 with the 1.5pm service from Penzance to Liverpool. The 'Warship' is painted in the standard BR maroon livery that was applied to most members of the class. This service also carried mail, the first three vehicles on the service comprising a Travelling Post Office vehicle and two parcels vans. No D813 was withdrawn from Newton Abbot in January 1972. *GWT/PAF*

Above right:
The 33 North British 'Warships' (Class 43) were fitted with two NBL/MAN 12-cylinder engines, each developing 1,100bhp. No 853 *Thruster*, built in August 1961, passes Didcot via the East Loop in May 1971 with a service from Hereford to Paddington. The engine is in plain BR blue livery with yellow ends and a single BR arrow totem placed under the nameplate. The D prefix has been removed from the number. This engine was involved in a high-speed derailment at Didcot while working a Paddington to Bristol service on

27 September 1967. It was withdrawn from Newton Abbot in October 1971. *Author*

Below right:
The railway works at Swindon was an interesting place during the late 1950s with steam locomotives ('9F' class 2-10-0 freight engines) being built alongside the new diesel-hydraulic types. Steam construction finished at Swindon in January 1960, and with the completion of the last Swindon-built 'Warship', No D870 *Zulu* in September 1961, attention turned to the new class of main-line diesels known as the 'Westerns'. This type again used the diesel-hydraulic system, but with lessons learned from the 'Warships', proved to be much more reliable in service. The Type 4 (later Class 52) 'Westerns' were powered by two Maybach engines each developing 1,350bhp. Construction was shared between Swindon and Crewe, with Nos D1000-D1029 built at Swindon and Nos D1030-D1074 at Crewe. These were the most successful of the hydraulics, with a number remaining in service for 15 years.

The Western Region was undecided about the livery to adopt for these new locomotives.

The first of the class, No D1000 *Western Enterprise* was turned out from Swindon in December 1961 in experimental 'desert sand'; No D1001 *Western Pathfinder*, which was constructed in January 1962, appeared in green livery, as did Nos D1002 *Western Explorer*, D1003 *Western Pioneer* and D1004 *Western Crusader*. Maroon livery was applied to No D1005 in June 1962, and yet another experiment saw No D1015 *Western Champion*, completed in January 1963, turned out in golden ochre. Interestingly, BR maroon became the standard livery for the 'Westerns', after the Western Region held a public vote to determine the most popular colour.

The first member of the class, No D1000 *Western Enterprise*, stands at Paddington on 24 March 1963, finished in desert sand livery with half yellow ends and a large chrome-plated British Transport totem on the cab side. Notice the trail of steam from the train heating boiler. The 'Westerns' were eventually painted, first in maroon and then later in BR blue. No D1000 was withdrawn from service at Plymouth Laira in February 1974. *GWT/CGS*

Left:
As already mentioned, another experimental livery was golden ochre, seen here on No D1015 *Western Champion*, as it stands outside Swindon shed (82C) on 23 February 1964. The engine has half yellow ends and the circular BR crest-type emblem. Built at Swindon in January 1963, No D1015 was withdrawn from Laira in December 1976. It has since been preserved in main-line running order by the Diesel Traction Group. *GWT/PAF*

Above:
The first batch of 'Westerns' built at Crewe, Nos D1035-D1038, were also turned out in the very attractive green livery, seen here on No D1036 *Western Emperor* as it passes West Ealing with a race special from Paddington to Cheltenham on 14 March 1963. The train is formed of BR Mk1 stock, except for the last but one coach, which is the ex-Great Western Royal Saloon conveying HM The Queen Mother to the races. No D1036 was built at Crewe in August 1962, and withdrawn from Laira in November 1976. *GWT/CGS*

THE DIESEL-HYDRAULICS

Right:
The 'Westerns' were initially put on services over the 'cut-off' route between Paddington, Birmingham and Wolverhampton. Standing at Wolverhampton Low Level on 18 July 1960, after arrival with a service from Paddington, is 'Castle' class 4-6-0 No 5031 *Totnes Castle* and 'Western' No D1005 *Western Venturer*. This was the first Class 52 to be painted in maroon livery. No 5031 was built at Swindon in May 1934 and withdrawn from Wolverhampton Stafford Road in October 1963, while No D1005 was withdrawn from Laira in November 1976. *GWT/CGS*

Below:
As mentioned previously, maroon was eventually adopted by the Western Region for all its main-line diesels. This livery can be seen to good effect on No D1014 *Western Leviathan* as it speeds past North Acton with the 4.10pm service to Birmingham on 13 April 1963. The 'Westerns' looked good in maroon as long as they were kept clean. No D1014 was built at Swindon in December 1962 and withdrawn in August 1974. *GWT/CGS*

Above:

Towards the end of their working lives many of the surviving Class 52s were used on freight services. On 7 June 1975, No D1055 *Western Advocate*, in the BR blue livery that was eventually applied to all of the class, passes White Waltham with down milk empties from Kensington to St Erth. Built by BR at Crewe in March 1963, No D1055 was withdrawn from Plymouth Laira in January 1976. Although included in the TOPS scheme, because of their cast numberplates the 'Westerns' were not renumbered into that system. *GWT/MY*

Left:

Probably the least successful of the diesel-hydraulics were the 1,100bhp North British Locomotive Type 2 B-Bs (Class 22). Nos D6300-D6357 were introduced between 1959 and 1962, and from new saw use in the South West of England. There, they could be used in multiple on main-line services, or singly on branch passenger and goods services. With the closure of many West Country branch lines, and the non-availability of spares (the North British Company went into liquidation during 1962), many were withdrawn after less than 10 years' service. In later years, a number were allocated to Old Oak Common where they were used on light freight and empty stock duties. Pictured entering Bodmin Road station on 27 April 1962, with a goods service from Wadebridge, is No D6314. It has full green ends and train description discs. Delivered in January 1960, it was withdrawn from Laira in April 1969. *GWT/CGS*

Above:
The Beyer Peacock 'Hymek' Type 3 B-Bs (Class 35) were introduced by the Western Region during the summer of 1961. Built in Manchester, they were powered by a single Maybach MD870 engine giving 1,700bhp. A total of 101 'Hymeks' were constructed between 1961 and 1964. At first, the class was allocated to Bristol Bath Road and Cardiff Canton, but by the early 1970s, a number were also operating from Old Oak Common. The class soon displaced steam on services to and from South Wales and also from Paddington to Worcester and Hereford, which until 1964 were still being operated with 'Castle' class 4-6-0s. After some teething problems the 'Hymeks'

performed well, but reliability was always a problem, with the Mekydro transmissions prone to a number of faults. In later years, just like the other diesel-hydraulic classes, the supply of parts became a problem, and many locomotives were withdrawn after only 10 years of service.

No D7010, built in November 1961, is seen here departing from Didcot with the 8.50am service from Taunton to Paddington on 27 March 1962. It is in the original dark and light green livery with grey cab window surrounds and red bufferbeams. Notice the ex-GWR wooden up starting signal on the platform. No D7010 was withdrawn from Bristol Bath Road in November 1972. *GWT/CGS*

Left:
From January 1962, all 'Hymeks' were turned out with half yellow ends, as seen in this view of No D7021 at Swindon MPD on 7 August 1962. Built in February 1962, this locomotive was withdrawn from Bristol Bath Road in June 1972. *GWT/CGS*

Below:
Pictured here arriving at Newport in July 1962 is 'Hymek' No D7031 with the 1.55pm service from Paddington to Pembroke Dock. The diesel is in trouble, having broken down en route, and has been rescued by a pair of ex-Great Western locomotives in the form of '5205' class 2-8-0T No 5243 and '5101' class 2-6-2 No 4145, both from Severn Tunnel Junction (86E). Not a particularly fast part of the journey, one would think. No D7031 was withdrawn from Old Oak Common in May 1973. *GWT/EM*

Above:
By the mid-1960s, the 'Hymeks' were being painted in BR blue livery with the corporate BR double arrow on the side, but still retaining the grey window frames. This livery is seen on No D7048 as it passes Handborough for Blenheim with a Hereford to Paddington via Oxford service on 15 March 1967. Built in September 1962, No D7048 was withdrawn from Old Oak Common in January 1972. Handborough was opened in 1854 as Handborough Junction when the Oxford, Worcester & Wolverhampton Railway operated its service between Worcester and Euston. The wooden station building on the right probably dates from around that period. *GWT/CGS*

Above right:
Another diesel-hydraulic type constructed for the Western Region at Swindon was the BR Type 1 (Class 14) 0-6-0s. In all, 56 members of the class were built between July 1964 and October 1965. These small, 650hp locomotives were used for shunting duties and trip working and were generally quite successful when introduced, but the Beeching cuts of the period saw many of the branch lines and yards closed, which meant the class was made more or less redundant from the start. A number then saw use on the North Eastern Region, but this work also dwindled away, and by April 1969, all had been withdrawn from service on BR. Most went into industrial use, and many have since been preserved. Pictured here passing Cardiff General with a Cardiff to Llantrisant freight is No D9518. Built at Swindon in October 1964, it was one of the last to remain in BR service, being withdrawn in April 1969. It was subsequently sold to the National Coal Board for use at Ashington Colliery and is now preserved at the Rutland Railway Museum. *GWT/REM*

OTHER MOTIVE POWER

Above:
One might be excused for thinking that Swindon built only diesel-hydraulic types, but that was certainly not the case, as between 1957 and 1961, some 147 diesel-mechanical D2000-series (later Class 03) 204bhp 0-6-0 shunters were completed in the works. Fitted with a Gardner engine and a Drewry gearbox these diminutive engines saw use over most parts of the Western Region, and also BR as a whole. No D2087 was built at Swindon in June 1959, and is seen here in unlined green livery in the works yard on 7 August 1962. It was not allocated a TOPS number and was withdrawn from Landore in June 1971. *GWT/CGS*

Left:
The most numerous class of diesel shunters were the '08s'. Introduced by BR in October 1952, some 1,192 of these diesel-electric 0-6-0s were built and operated over the whole of the BR network. Surprisingly, none were built at Swindon, but the first five, Nos D3000-D3004, which were built at Derby in 1952, went straight to the Western Region, being allocated to Tyseley (84E). No D3359 was built at Derby in June 1957, and is seen here in Swindon shed yard after a works overhaul on 7 August 1962. The '08s' were at first turned out in black livery, but by the 1960s many were being painted in BR green. No D3359 was allocated to Llanelly (87F) when new; it was renumbered 08289 under the TOPS scheme in February 1974, and withdrawn from Derby in December 1985. *GWT/CGS*

Right:
In 1985, three Landore-based Class 08 shunters were fitted with cut-down cabs for working the Burry Port & Gwendraeth Valley line from Llanelli to Cwm Mawr. These replaced three Swindon-built Drewry Class 03 shunters that had worked the line for a number of years. The first '08' to be converted at Landore was No 08592 in July 1985 (previously No D3759, built at Crewe in October 1959). The cab height was reduced to 11ft 10in and it was renumbered 08993, as seen here at Llanelli, shortly after conversion, on 6 July 1985. It was named *Ashburton* on 1 January 1986. *David Parker*

Above:
In 1962, the Birmingham Railway Carriage & Wagon Co built a demonstrator Type 4 Co-Co diesel-electric fitted with a 2,750bhp Sulzer engine. No D0260 *Lion* underwent trials on the Western Region from March 1962. Allocated to 84A Plymouth Laira, it is seen here at Paddington waiting to leave with a service to Wolverhampton on 17 May 1962. It was painted in white livery with its nameplates mounted high up on the sides. After use on the Western Region it was loaned to the Eastern Region and allocated to 34G Finsbury Park, from where it was withdrawn in October 1963. It was cut up just one month later.
GWT/CGS

Left:
Another demonstration locomotive was the Brush Type 4 Co-Co *Falcon*. Built at Loughborough in 1961, it was powered by two Maybach engines each developing 1,440bhp and worked on both the Western and Eastern Regions. It is seen here on a down parcels service at West Ealing on 24 February 1962. The locomotive is in light green livery, with a darker green frame line and window surrounds. It was quite successful and was taken into BR stock in December 1970 and renumbered D1200. After some years on the Western Region it was withdrawn from Newport Ebbw Junction in October 1975. *GWT/CGS*

Lower left:
The Brush diesel-electric Type 4s (later Class 47) were introduced on Western Region services in October 1963. Powered by a 2,580bhp Sulzer engine the first locomotives were allocated to Old Oak Common and Bristol, but later batches went to Newport and Landore. From 1964, the Class 47s replaced the 'Western' Class 52s on many of the services between Paddington and Wolverhampton. The '47s' proved to be good machines, and as more and more were delivered they took over many of the diesel-hydraulic turns.

Brush Type 4 No D1698 was built by Brush at Loughborough in December 1963 and is seen here at Leamington Spa on a driver-training special on 20 March 1964. The locomotive is as delivered in two-tone green livery with half yellow ends. Allocated from new to 81A Old Oak Common, it was renumbered 47110 in February 1974, and withdrawn from Sheffield Tinsley in May 1989. *GWT/CGS*

Upper right:
Seen here in plain BR blue livery, Class 47 No D1674 *Samson* stands at Penzance on 24 May 1970 with the up 'Cornish Riviera Express', the 10.05 service from Penzance to Paddington. The train comprises just six BR Mk1 coaches as additional coaches will be added at Plymouth. Built by BR at Crewe in May 1965, No D1674 has carried no fewer than five different numbers since new: it was renumbered to 47088 in February 1974, 47653 in August 1986, 47808 in February 1989 and 47781 in March 1994. It was finally withdrawn from service during 2004 and at the time of writing was in store. The blue and grey livery was first introduced by the Western Region on 18 April 1966.

The station at Penzance was opened by the West Cornwall Railway on 11 March 1853. It was enlarged by the Great Western in 1939 to provide four platforms, but today only three remain in use. *GWT/PAF*

Above:
The Brush Type 2 (Class 31) diesel-electrics were first introduced in 1957. Originally built for the Eastern Region, during 1969 a number were reallocated to the Western Region at Old Oak Common where they first saw use on empty stock trains in and out of Paddington. The '31s' proved to be useful engines, and were employed on both freight and passenger services in the London and Bristol areas. After withdrawal of the 'Hymeks', Old Oak Common-based Class 31s were used for a number of years on services between Paddington and Worcester.

Class 31 No 31260 is seen here in BR blue with full yellow ends on a short engineers' train at Twyford, Berkshire, on 16 April 1974. The train comprises a concrete wagon, a four-wheel steel ballast wagon and a brake van. Built by Brush as No D5688 in February 1961 and allocated to Sheffield Darnall, it was renumbered in February 1964, and after several years' use on the Western Region, was returned to the North East, being withdrawn from Thornaby in January 1990. *GWT/MY*

Above:
Built by the English Electric Company at the Vulcan Foundry, the Type 4 Class 50s were initially introduced on London Midland Region West Coast main-line services during 1967/68. Numbered in the D400 series, all were turned out from new in BR blue livery. They were renumbered as Class 50s under the TOPS scheme during 1973/74. The completion of the electrification on the WCML north of Crewe saw them transferred to the Western Region during 1974. In 1978, and in true Great Western/Western Region fashion the whole of the class were named after Royal Navy warships. They were soon to be found on all of the Western Region main-line services, essentially displacing the remaining Class 52 'Westerns'.

Passing through Frome with the diverted 07.55 service from Paignton to Paddington on 16 April 1977 is Class 50 No 50004, then unnamed and in BR blue livery with small cabside numbers and centre BR double arrow logo. It was named *St Vincent* in May 1978. Built in December 1967 as No D404, it was renumbered in February 1974 and withdrawn from Plymouth Laira in June 1990. *GWT/PAF*

Above left:
Soon after the Class 50s were named, the double arrow logo was moved to the side of the cab at the opposite end to the number, as seen on No 50007 *Hercules*, as it passes through Pewsey station with the 08.34 service from Penzance to Paddington on 7 April 1980. In February 1984, No 50007 was renamed *Sir Edward Elgar* and repainted in Great Western style lined-green livery. The only member of the class to receive this livery, it was built as No D407 in March 1968 and was renumbered in April 1974. It was withdrawn from service in 1991, and is currently preserved at the Midland Railway — Butterley. *GWT/PAF*

Above:
The brass nameplate of *Sir Edward Elgar* and Great Western crest as carried by Class 50 No 50007, photographed in July 1984. The nameplate was fitted to commemorate the 50th anniversary of Elgar's death in 1934. Notice the GW-style green livery and lining applied to this locomotive. *Author*

Right:
During 1985, the livery on the Class 50s was changed once again. The yellow ends were extended back to cover the cab doors, and a large number, and an even larger double-arrow logo, were placed on each side of the nameplate. This livery can be seen to good effect on No 50028 *Tiger* as it emerges from Parsons Tunnel with a down service from Paddington to Plymouth on 5 August 1985. Built in July 1968, No 50028 was withdrawn from Plymouth Laira in January 1991. *GWT/PAF*

Above:
Although not operated solely by the Western Region, many cross-country services passed through the region on a daily basis. One such service was the 'Cornishman', the 10.5am service from Penzance to Leeds City. This service was originally introduced by the Western Region in 1952 and ran between Wolverhampton Low Level and Penzance via Stratford upon Avon. In 1962 the service was extended through to Leeds and ran via Gloucester and Birmingham New Street. The up service, here comprising 12 coaches, is seen at Dainton Bank on 16 September 1974, hauled by BR Type 4 'Peak' Class 46 No 46012. A number of Class 46s were allocated to Plymouth Laira (84A) specifically for working these through inter-regional services. The small brick building on the left, centre, is Dainton Siding signalbox, which was closed on 14 February 1965. *GWT/PAF*

Above:

Perhaps the biggest ever change to passenger services on the Western Region was the introduction during 1976 of the new Class 253, InterCity 125 High Speed Trains. Capable of speeds of up to 125mph, they transformed services to the South West, Bristol and South Wales. Prior to their introduction, a prototype Class 252, No 252001, was tested on services between Paddington and Bristol. It is seen here passing Ealing Broadway on 6 June 1975, with the 16.45 down service to Bristol. The set was painted in grey and blue livery with yellow ends. One of the main differences between the '252' prototype and the production '253' power cars (now Class 43) was the smaller oblong central cab window. One of the power cars from this set has since been preserved in the National Railway Museum, York. *GWT/CGS*

Above:

When the Class 253s were introduced on Western Region services they carried the new corporate livery of blue and light grey with InterCity 125 logos on the power cars. This livery can be seen to good effect here as No 253007 passes Taplow on 28 December 1976 with an up Bristol service. Notice the larger cab window and the addition of a cab side window, fitted on all production power cars. On 30 August 1984, records were broken when an HST ran between Paddington and Bristol in just 62 minutes and 33 seconds — an average speed of 112.8mph. *GWT/MY*

DIESEL MULTIPLE-UNITS

Below:
The South West was the first area on the Western Region to be dieselised. This is well illustrated in this picture of Fowey, the terminus of the short branch from Lostwithiel. The station is pictured here on 16 June 1962, and standing in the platform after arriving with the passenger service from Lostwithiel is Gloucester RC&WCo No W55001. These single-car DMUs were cheap to run and were ideal for this type of branch line, and at peak times the service could easily be strengthened with the addition of a trailer car. Waiting to work back to St Blazey with its solitary brake van is North British Type 2 No D6319. The Type 2s were used on many of the goods services in the South West area.

The branch from Lostwithiel to Fowey was opened as a mineral railway on 1 June 1869. It closed on 1 January 1880 but was reopened by the Great Western on 16 September 1895. Fowey was the principal china clay port in Cornwall, so the branch became very busy with this traffic. Dieselisation did not save the passenger services and it was closed to passengers on 4 January 1965. Today, what remains of the branch, which now terminates at Carne Point, is still in use for china clay traffic.
GWT/PAF

Right:
The Derby-built three-car suburban units (Class 116) were introduced by the Western Region on services between Cardiff and Treherbert on 11 September 1957, and extended to cover all Cardiff Valley line services on 13 January 1958. A Class 116 unit is seen here at Cardiff Queen Street on a service to Barry Island in around 1959. The set is in green livery with a half yellow warning strip, and the cab roof is painted white with a high-level route identification light above the destination blind.

Cardiff Queen Street was built in 1887 on the site of the earlier Taff Vale Railway station. The overall roof was removed during 1974 when the station was demolished and rebuilt as an island platform with a single bay. The new station was opened on 17 July 1975.
GWT/EM

Above:
The Swindon-built Class 120/1 and 120/2 three-car cross-country units were introduced in 1957 and were some of the first DMUs to run on the Western Region. Powered by a pair of Leyland six-cylinder diesel engines developing 150bhp, they initially went into general use on services between Bristol, Cardiff and Birmingham. I can remember them, when new, being used for crew training between Oxford and Birmingham. Pictured here is one of these sets in the later BR blue and grey livery, headed by Driving Motor Brake Composite No W50727, entering Cheltenham Spa Lansdown with a service from Cardiff to Birmingham on 25 March 1968. *GWT/CGS*

Above right:
During 1961 Swindon built a further batch of Class 120, three-car cross-country sets. Depicted at Tiverton Junction on 15 November 1962, is Driving Motor Second No W51584 at the rear of the Exeter

to Taunton stopping service. The power car is in original condition with a four-digit train description panel, green livery and half yellow ends. *GWT/CGS*

Lower right:
In 1958, the Western Region ordered a number of single-car Driving Motor Brake Second DMUs for branch services. The first batch of 20 (Class 122s) were built by the Gloucester Railway Carriage & Wagon Company. The units were non-gangwayed and had side doors to each seating bay. Seen here arriving at Much Wenlock on 21 July 1962 — just two days before the service was withdrawn — is unit No W55009 with the 5.45pm service from Wellington. With the poor patronage on some of the branches these single-car units were probably all that was needed, although the reduced running costs still did not save many such lines. The station building at Much Wenlock survives and has been converted into private housing. *GWT/PAF*

Above:
Sixteen single-car Driving Motor Brake Seconds (Class 121) were built for the Western Region by the Pressed Steel Co. These units were fitted with route identification panels above the cab windows, but apart from this they were essentially identical to the Gloucester units. Standing at Windsor & Eton Central on 30 August 1962, with a service to Paddington, is car No W55022 with a trailer car. The unit has the early type of 'cat's whiskers' yellow warning stripe on the cab. Today, Windsor & Eton Central has been reduced to just one platform, with the area in the picture covered by a shopping arcade. A number of Class 121s have been preserved, with some others in Departmental use. *GWT/CGS`*

Left:
The Gloucester Railway Carriage & Wagon Co 128 Driving Motor Parcels Vans were introduced 1959. Powered by two 230bhp Leyland Albion engines, nine were built, and the Western Region operated two: Nos W55991 and W55992. They replaced the two ex-Great Western parcels railcars Nos W17W and W34W. No W55991 is seen here Southall on 10 November 1963, fitted with end gangways, reporting number panels, and is in pl green livery with yellow coach lines. The BR er has been placed on the centre door. *GWT/CGS*

Above:
In later years, the parcel van units were painted in BR blue. Seen here passing Ruscombe on 21 June 1975 with an up parcels service, comprising a GUV, a single DMU power car and a variety of other vans is unit No W55992. The unit number has been moved to a more central position, with two BR arrow totems at each end. The single DMU power car also has 'Parcels Service' painted on the side. *GWT/MY*

Below:
A pair of Gloucester RC&WCo Class 119 cross-country units stand at Reading with an up service from Frome to Paddington on 10 August 1962. The front vehicle is Driving Motor Brake Composite No W51066. These units, powered by two AEC six-cylinder engines developing 150bhp, were introduced by the Western Region in 1958. The driving unit is fitted with a central two-figure route identification panel, a top destination panel which appears to be empty, and it has a half yellow cab. The centre front window carries a Paddington sticker. *GWT/CGS*

Left:
The '119' class DMUs were later painted in BR blue and grey with full yellow ends; set numbers were introduced by the Western Region in the early 1970s. Seen here passing through Sydney Gardens, Bath, with a service from Salisbury to Bristol on 24 June 1976, is Bristol-based set No B573, with No W51055 leading. *GWT/CGS*

Above:
The Pressed Steel Company also built a number of three-car Class 117 suburban units for the Western Region. These were introduced in 1959 and were powered by a pair of Leyland 150bhp engines. They were gangwayed with side doors to each seating bay and were first introduced on the local Thames Valley services during 1960. Entering Didcot, with a service from Oxford to Paddington on 27 March 1963, is a three-car set headed by No W51395. The unit is in green with grey cab top, route numbers and yellow V 'cat's whiskers' warning stripes. *GWT/CGS*

Above:
Another Class 117 unit, No 51360 (fitted with half buffers) stands at Uxbridge Vine Street on 25 August 1962 with the 5.44pm service to West Drayton & Yiewsley. A Scammell 'mechanical horse' can be seen in the goods yard. The West Drayton to Uxbridge branch was opened on 8 September 1856, and was closed to passenger traffic on 10 September 1962 and to goods on 24 February 1964. The '117s' certainly gave good service, continuing to work on Thames Valley suburban services for over 30 years until replaced by the Class 165 Turbo units in 1993. *GWT/PAF*

Right:
For longer distances, Swindon Works constructed a number of Class 123 Inter-City units. Introduced in 1963, they were powered by a pair of Leyland six-cylinder engines developing 230bhp which gave them a good turn of speed. Originally, they were formed as four-car sets, but over the years some were reduced to three cars. Initially, they operated services between South Wales, Bristol, Plymouth and the Midlands. However, by the 1970s, a number had been transferred to the Eastern Region, with the remainder operating out of Paddington, usually on services to and from Oxford. Seen here passing Taplow on 19 January 1974 are two four-car sets headed by No L706 on the 13.10 service to Oxford. *GWT/MY*

Left:
Even the absence of a steam train does not reduce the appeal of a country station. Avoncliff Halt is situated on the line from Bathampton to Bradford-on-Avon and was opened by the Great Western on 24 August 1906. The wooden shelters were a later addition. The line at this point follows the course of the River Avon (right) and the Kennet & Avon Canal through the valley. Looking down from the aqueduct bridge, which carries the canal over the line at this point, a three-car cross-country unit arrives with the 2.10pm service from Weymouth to Bristol. The unit is in BR blue with half yellow ends and white cab roofs. *GWT/PAF*

Above:
During the early 1980s, the Western Region replaced a number of the older DMUs on services in the South West with Class 142 'Pacer' four-wheeled railbuses. Set No 142023 is seen here on a Newquay to Par service near Roche on 30 June 1986, painted in chocolate and cream livery. The '142s' were known as 'Skippers' in the South West, but they soon proved to be unsuitable for these services due mainly to slipping and excess flange wear because of the tight curves on these lines. They were subsequently replaced by Class 150/153 'Sprinters'. *David Parker*

Left:
A Pressed Steel three-car Class 117 set, strengthened with an extra trailer car, crosses Pensford Viaduct on the Bristol to Frome line on 6 April 1968 with an RCTS special from Paddington to Portishead. The service traversed a number of closed freight and branch lines in the Bristol area. The viaduct which is now a listed structure was opened on 3 September 1873. The Bristol to Frome line was closed to passengers on 2 November 1959 and as a through route for freight on 10 June 1963. *GWT/PAF*

Above right:
Also in the early 1980s, the Western Region introduced two experimental Class 210 diesel-electric units on some Thames Valley services. These were built at Derby in 1981 and were fitted with Paxman and MTU engines and had air-operated sliding doors. The first prototype, No 210001, was a four-car set with Paxman engines, and is seen at Radley on a service from Oxford to Reading on 20 February 1984. It is in standard BR blue and grey with yellow ends. Both units were withdrawn in around 1987/88 with the coaches being reused, some for Departmental duties, others as EMU trailer cars. *David Parker*

FREIGHT SERVICES

Freight services during the early years of the Western Region had changed little from the days of the Great Western. The service still mainly comprised fast fitted freights that ran at night, the slower, long-distance loads over the main lines, and short pick-up goods along secondary lines and branches. Coal was still an important commodity, and in 1913 there were some 600 rail-connected collieries in South Wales. The gradual decline of the coal industry saw the number of collieries reduced and, with the rapid decline of the 1960s and '70s, there is now only one rail-connected colliery left in South Wales. The closure and rundown of many lines during the 1960s also saw a change in the way freight was moved. In many areas, road took over from rail, local goods yards were closed and the branch-line goods service almost disappeared, although the Western Region continued to provide what were probably unremunerative services over a number of lines that had lost their passenger services some years earlier. However, it was not all bad news, for in 1960 the Western Region opened a new marshalling yard at Margam in South Wales. The introduction of fast long-distance air-braked, block and company trains saw a rapid reduction in the use of older wagons, many of which were built by the Great Western.

Above left:
The ex-Great Western '2800/2884' class 2-8-0s were the mainstay of Western Region freight services well into the 1960s. These Churchward-designed 2-8-0s could pull the heaviest of trains. Here, '2884' class No 3843 hauls an up mixed freight service through Kemble on 25 November 1961. It was built at Swindon in February 1942 and was withdrawn in October 1963. On the far left is AC Cars four-wheel railbus No W79977 on a Tetbury branch service. In the centre of the picture is the station water tower, well head and pumping house. *GWT/PAF*

Above right:
Fowey was, and still is, an important centre for the movement of china clay. The old branch now terminates at Carne Point but is still used for china clay traffic to and from the docks. Today, the clay is carried in modern wagons, but it was not until the 1980s that these were introduced. Prior to this, china clay was carried in wooden wagons using a design that dated back to GWR days. This five-plank design can be seen here in this picture of ex-Great Western 0-6-0PT No 9716 shunting at Fowey on 22 April 1961. Nearest the locomotive is Shell fuel wagon No 4507, its black tank indicating that it is suitable for Class B traffic (inflammable). The china clay wagon that can be identified is No B743383, which was built by BR at Swindon in 1955. Also in view is a typical ex-GWR shunter's truck. Notice, also, the disused capstan and winch in the foreground, once used for moving wagons around the yard. *GWT/CGS*

Lower right:
Ex-Great Western 'Hall' class 4-6-0 No 4908 *Broome Hall* passes through Leamington Spa on 29 May 1963 with a down freight, probably bound for Bordesley yard. The headlamp code designates this as a fast freight containing perishables or livestock. Many of these fast freight services travelled at night. The engine is minus its shed allocation plate and is coupled to a standard ex-GWR 4,000-gallon tender. No 4908 was built in January 1929, and was withdrawn only a few months after this picture was taken, in October 1963. *GWT/CGS*

Above:

A superb scenic view of ex-Great Western '5700' class pannier tank No 9607 on the 3pm Nantymoel to Tondu goods service at Rhondda Main Colliery near Ogmore Vale on 18 October 1963. Coal was an important commodity for the railway, with almost every pit in South Wales served by the GWR and later the Western Region. Widespread pit closures in South Wales over the last 30 years have resulted in only Tower Colliery still being rail connected. No 9607 was built at Swindon in June 1945, and withdrawn in March 1964. *GWT/CGS*

Left:

Another coal train, hauled by ex-Great Western 0-6-2T No 5626, runs down off the old Rhymney Railway Walnut Tree branch at Taff's Well on 18 September 1963. The 0-6-2Ts proved to be ideal engines for valley services, being used for both passenger and goods work. Many of the class lasted until the end of steam in South Wales. No 5626 is seen here in unlined black livery with the old-style BR lion and wheel emblem. It was built at Swindon in August 1925, and after spending the whole of its working life in South Wales, was withdrawn from service in December 1963. *GWT/PAF*

Right:

The Western Region operated a number of LMS-designed '8F' 2-8-0s which it inherited from the Great Western. Designed by Stanier in 1935, 80 of these 2-8-0s were built at Swindon during 1943 and 1944. On 10 August 1962, No 48431, which was built at Swindon in 1944, passes Wantage Road with some down coal empties. The engine is in unlined black and carries an 82B, Bristol St Philip's Marsh shedplate. Notice that the newer, all-steel wagons are interspersed with what appear to be some ex-Great Western eight-plank coal wagons.

The large building in the background is the stationmaster's house and station entrance. Wantage Road was closed to passengers on 7 December 1964 and, today, nothing remains of the old station. After withdrawal, No 48431 ended up at Woodhams' yard at Barry, but has since been preserved on the Keighley & Worth Valley Railway. *GWT/CGS*

Below:

Another typical Western Region pick-up goods service operated over the old Wycombe Railway branch between Maidenhead, Marlow and High Wycombe. The service is seen here at Bourne End on 20 March 1962, being shunted by '9400' class 0-6-0PT No 9406. All but the first 10 of the class were built by outside contractors, many long after Nationalisation. No 9406 is in unlined black with later type BR emblem. It was built at Swindon in May 1947 and was withdrawn in September 1964. The line from Bourne End to High Wycombe was closed on 4 May 1970 and the branch now terminates at Bourne End station (left), where passenger services from Marlow now reverse. *GWT/CGS*

Left:
New and old together as a brand-new English Electric Type 3 (Class 37), No D6833, and ex-Great Western '4300' class 2-6-0 No 6347 enter Conwil station on 20 May 1963 with a goods working from Carmarthen to Lampeter. The Type 3s were delivered to Cardiff Canton in April 1963 and were first used on the Newport Dock to Llanwern ore trains. Eventually, they took over many of the freight services in South Wales. No D6833 was built at the Vulcan Foundry in April 1963, it was renumbered 37133 in May 1964 and is, at the time of writing, withdrawn and in store at Carnforth, Lancashire. The Mogul was built at Swindon in April 1923 and was withdrawn in December 1963. Passenger services were withdrawn between Carmarthen and Lampeter on 22 February 1965, and goods services on 22 September 1973. *GWT/MY*

Above:
Parcels traffic was an important revenue earner for the railways. Passing through Reading on 10 August 1962 is an up parcels service from the South West hauled by Bristol-based ex-Great Western 'County' class 4-6-0 No 1024 *County of Pembroke*. The engine carries the C headcode which denotes a parcels train fitted throughout with automatic vacuum brakes. A variety of stock can be seen, including what appears to be an ex-LNER Gresley parcels van. Originally painted in lined black livery, No 1024 is seen here in BR lined-green livery, but in a grubby condition. It was withdrawn from service in April 1964. *GWT/CGS*

Right:
Towards the end of their life, many of the 'Castle' class 4-6-0s had been displaced from passenger duties and were being used on fast freight services. Passing Chalford station on its climb up to Sapperton on 3 October 1964 is No 7013 *Bristol Castle* pulling hard with an up freight service; it is banked at the rear by ex-GWR '6100' class 2-6-2T No 6113. The headlamp code denotes a fast freight service not fitted with continuous brakes. No 7013 was actually No 4082 *Windsor Castle*, built at Swindon in 1924, the two locomotives swapping identities in February 1952 when No 4082 was not available to haul King George VI's funeral train. They were never swapped back and the two 'Castles' retained their false identities, with the older locomotive being withdrawn in February 1965. *GWT/MY*

Below:
Aggregate traffic from the Somerset quarries was an important feature of Western Region freight services. Passing Froxfield, Wiltshire, on 17 May 1976 with a heavy aggregate train from Foster Yeoman's Merehead Quarry to Acton Yard is Class 52 No D1010 *Western Campaigner*. The engine is in BR blue with full yellow ends, and at this time the few remaining 'Westerns' were mainly being used for freight work. Notice the train recording numbers are in use as a front numberplate, showing No 1010. This locomotive was withdrawn from service in February 1977 and is now preserved on the West Somerset Railway. Today, the heavy aggregate trains of Hanson and Foster Yeoman are operated by Mendip Rail and EWS General Motors Class 59 and EWS Class 60 locomotives. *GWT/MY*

The Class 47s were true mixed traffic locomotives and operated passenger and freight services over the whole of the country, including many inter-regional services. They were first introduced on Western Region passenger services in 1963, but as more and more were delivered they were also used on freight traffic. Passing Ruscombe on 9 September 1975 is No 47229 with a down mixed freight service from the Midlands. Built by Brush at Loughborough in September 1965 as No D1905 and allocated to Cardiff Canton, it was renumbered in the TOPS series in October 1973. *GWT/MY*

Above:
Another inter-regional freight from the North West to South Wales was the 08.35 service from Carlisle to Severn Tunnel Junction, seen here hauled by an unidentified BR Type 4 (Class 46) as it approaches Pontrilas on the ex-Great Western Hereford to Newport line, on 26 April 1975. The line on the left is the remains of the Golden Valley branch to Hay-on-Wye, which was closed in 1957. The once-busy Severn Tunnel Junction yard is now closed and has been covered by the toll booths of the Second Severn Crossing road bridge. The Newport to Hereford line still forms an important cross-country freight route. *GWT/MY*

LOCOMOTIVE DEPOTS

As already mentioned, the formation of the Western Region in 1948 initially appeared to be nothing more than a name change to the many workers of the old Great Western Railway. Steam still reigned supreme on the region at this time and the locomotive depot was an important part of the infrastructure, right up until the end of Western Region steam traction in 1965. The 1955 modernisation programme took time to implement, and even in 1959, steam still accounted for some 95% of the Western Region's motive power. At this time, there were 66 main steam sheds and 62 sub sheds still in operation on the region.

There were many designs of engine shed on the Great Western, but it was Churchward who, in 1901, introduced a standard locomotive shed design, using brick construction with a slate roof. This ideal did not last for long as the Grouping in 1923 brought a number of smaller companies into the Great Western system, and with them a variety of locomotive sheds.

Above:
Moorswater shed was opened by the Liskeard & Looe Railway in 1868. The two-road stone-built structure is seen here in the late 1950s; on the left is the combined coaling platform and water tower. Standing alongside is ex-Great Western 2-6-2T No 5553, still in black livery with the lion and wheel emblem.

Built at Swindon in 1928, No 5553 was withdrawn in November 1961. The building just in view in the left background was the old L&LR locomotive works and wagon shops. In Great Western and Western Region days Moorswater was a sub shed of St Blazey, and was closed in September 1960. *GWT*

Above:
This view of Severn Tunnel Junction shed was taken on 25 June 1963. Locomotives on view are ex-Great Western 'Modified Hall' class 4-6-0 No 6973 *Bricklehampton Hall*, '4200' class 2-8-0T No 4296 and a variety of other types. The shed at this time was still predominantly steam, although one of the new English Electric Type 3 diesel-electrics can be seen on the right. The building illustrates the standard Churchward design and was opened in 1907. The brick-built structure originally contained four roads. In 1939, the shed was extended to six roads, the new section visible on the right. During World War 2 a standard GW-design asbestos-clad repair shop was added (far left). Severn Tunnel Junction was coded 86E by the Western Region. In 1959, it had an allocation of 73 steam engines, of which 25 were ex-Great Western '2800' class 2-8-0s. The shed was closed in October 1965. *GWT/CGS*

Above:
A similar type of shed was built at Westbury in 1915. This four-road through shed was also constructed of brick, and was built to allow for future extension, but which never actually took place. On the right is the large lifting shop and shed offices. Locomotives on view here, on 25 December 1961 are, from left to right: '5400' class 0-6-0PT No 5416, 'Hall' and 'Modified Hall' class 4-6-0s Nos 4933 *Himley Hall*, 7902 *Eaton Mascot Hall* and 4917 *Crosswood Hall*, '5700' class 0-6-0PT No 3629 and 'Hall' class No 5920 *Wycliffe Hall*. There were 52 engines allocated to Westbury in 1959, of which 13 were ex-Great Western 'Halls'. The shed was closed in September 1965. *GWT/PAF*

Left:
Many of the main depots had sub sheds, which were often situated at the end of branch lines or near junction stations and goods yards. This picture shows the sub shed at Frome on 25 December 1961, with four 0-6-0PTs present: Nos 4636, 4647, 9628 and 9769. Opened in 1890 as a sub shed of nearby Westbury, the single-road building was constructed of wood. This was a cheap method of construction, and was used for a number of sub sheds on the system. Many of these wooden sheds lasted well into Western Region days. Frome's closure was in September 1963. *GWT/PAF*

Right:
Living in Oxford, I just have to include this picture of my favourite locomotive shed, Oxford (81F). Standing outside the wooden engine shed on 11 July 1963 is 'Modified Hall' class 4-6-0 No 7900 *St Peter's Hall*. In 1963, there were 15 'Halls' allocated to Oxford. The shed was constructed by the Oxford, Worcester & Wolverhampton Railway in around 1854 and enlarged by the Great Western in 1866. Part of the 1866 extension can be seen here on 11 July 1963. Apart from a few minor alterations the shed remained basically unchanged until its closure to steam on 3 January 1966. I think that I am right in saying that Oxford was the only shed of its size never to have been either rebuilt or replaced during its working life, by either the Great Western or Western Region. No 7900 was built at Swindon by British Railways in April 1949. An Oxford engine for almost the whole of its working life, it was withdrawn in December 1964. One of its nameplates is now on display in St Peter's Hall, Oxford. *GWT/CGS*

Above:
During World War 2, the Great Western constructed a number of new, double-sided coaling plants. They were located at depots such as Oxford where the existing coaling plant was too low to accommodate locomotives with 4,000-gallon tenders. The new coaling plant at Oxford was constructed in November 1944 and is seen here on 11 July 1963. Standing under the coaling stage is ex-GWR '2884' class 2-8-0 No 2886, being coaled by hand using one of the small hopper wagons. The type of coal used by Great Western engines was soft and crushed easily, and as a result, the company did not construct any automated coaling plants. However, the coal being loaded here has been crushed into briquettes. *GWT/CGS*

Above:
One of the first steam locomotive depots to be dieselised by the Western Region was Plymouth Laira, but in this picture taken on 29 April 1962, steam is still very much in evidence. Laira was opened by the Great Western in 1901, and originally comprised a standard Churchward-designed 28-road roundhouse. A four-road straight shed, built under the 1929 Government Loans and Guarantees Act, was added in 1931. From about 1960, this new shed was used mainly for diesel maintenance, and can be seen on the left. The centre building is the depot stores, and the 1901 roundhouse is on the right. Locomotives in view from left to right are: 'Grange' class 4-6-0 No 6863 *Dolhywel Grange*, 'Castle' No 7022 *Hereford Castle*, 'Grange' No 6874 *Haughton Grange* and 'County' class 4-6-0 No 1003 *County of Wilts*. Laira was closed to steam in April 1964, and today an HST servicing depot stands on the site. *GWT/CGS*

Left:
St Blazey was opened by the GWR in around 1872 and comprised a brick-built half roundhouse containing nine roads served by a turntable. It was closed to steam in April 1962, but continued to be used as a diesel depot until 25 April 1987. The building, which is Grade 2 listed, is seen here in use as a diesel depot on 8 July 1984. Locomotives in view are Class 37 No 37273 and 'Peak' Class 45 No 45040. The main buildings are now in industrial use but the turntable is still in situ and forms part of the adjacent diesel depot. *David Parker*

Above:

The steam depot at Newport Ebbw Junction was closed in October 1965 and was replaced by a new diesel servicing depot which was situated alongside the South Wales main line. The new diesel shed, seen here on 30 May 1982, was a standard BR design, two-road building, a type that was used in many other locations throughout the country. Standing outside the shed is a pair of Class 08s, Nos 08781 and 08780, together with a number of Class 37s. During 1995, the depot was closed and demolished, and locomotives now stable at Newport station. *David Parker*

Above:

A view of the turntable at Old Oak Common in April 1983. The main shed building was demolished during March 1964, and in January 1965 a new three-road diesel servicing shed was brought into use. This was erected over the site of the old southern bay turntable. Old Oak Common was not officially closed to steam until 22 March 1965 when its few remaining serviceable engines moved down the line to Southall. Of the old layout only the western bay turntable was retained and is used as a locomotive stabling area. It is pictured here in April 1983 with Classes 31, 47 and 50 awaiting their next turns of duty. In the background is the refuelling shed and, on the left, the old steam repair shop. *Author*

Above:
With modern-day train speeds, track maintenance has become a high-tech job with many elaborate maintenance and tamping machines, but in the 1960s the local track gangs, particularly on branch lines, were still using basic equipment.

Pictured here, preparing to depart from Much Wenlock on 23 June 1963, is the local track gang. One of the gang is exchanging the single-line staff with the signalman. Their various tools are being carried on a platelayers' trolley which carries the number C14, and is hauled by four-wheel Wickham petrol trolley No B144W. These men had pride in their work and maintained their stretch of track to a high standard. This type of operation has now passed into history. *GWT/CGS*

ENGINEERING

Left:
The introduction of air-braked 'block' trains and the demise of the pick-up goods saw a rapid withdrawal of old rolling stock. However, a number of redundant vehicles were taken over by the engineering department where they saw further use. One of these was ex-GWR 20-ton brake van No W17399 seen here out of use at Princes Risborough on 7 April 1973. This was one of a batch of 100 brake vans built to Lot No 1370, Diagram AA21, that were constructed with government finance at Swindon, between November 1939 and December 1940. The four-wheel van is fitted with vacuum brakes and screw couplings and was classified as a 'Toad A'. *GWT/MY*

Above:
The use of old GWR coaches for engineering work continued on the Western Region well into the 1960s and '70s. Pictured here at Maidenhead on 22 October 1963 are four ex-Great Western vehicles in use as mobile accommodation for workers involved in the local resignalling scheme. From left to right are four-wheel ex-passenger stock Nos W9940W, W9948W and W9993W. The fourth vehicle is Clerestory Brake No W9978W. Many of the ex-GWR vehicles in preservation today survived only because of their use by the engineering department. *GWT/MY*

Above:
The Western Region operated a number of steam-operated breakdown cranes. These were strategically stationed around the region at Old Oak Common, Bristol Bath Road, Cardiff Canton, Landore and Plymouth Laira. The cranes were serviced at Swindon, and pictured here in the works yard on 24 March 1963 is 75-ton steam breakdown crane No A7. Built by Cowans & Sheldon to order No 85 at their Carlisle works in 1961, it was based at Swindon and is seen here as supplied in red livery with yellow lining. A second, similar 75-ton crane, order No 84, was also completed in 1961 and was allocated to Cardiff Canton. *GWT/CGS*

Left:
A short PW train hauled by BR Class 08 0-6-0DE No D3762, just visible, left, stands at West Ruislip on 23 June 1963. The centre vehicle is BR Western Region Engineering Department heavy-duty non-self-propelled 10-ton twin-jib crane No 275. Built by Taylor & Hubbard in 1953, it was withdrawn in March 1982. No D3762 was built at Crewe in December 1959, renumbered 08585 in March 1974 and is currently operated by Freightliner at Southampton Maritime. *GWT/CGS*

Above:
In 1959, the Western Region Civil Engineers' Department ordered five 0-6-0 diesel shunters for use in its permanent way yards. Built by Ruston & Hornsby at Lincoln, they were originally numbered PWM650-PWM654. Under the TOPS scheme they were designated Class 97/6 and renumbered accordingly. No 97651 (previously No PWM651) stands in the yard at Gloucester shed on 24 March 1985. It is in engineers' yellow livery with a red BR totem. After its withdrawal, No 97651 was heavily cannibalised for parts, but it has since been preserved and is now at the Northampton & Lamport Railway. *David Parker*

ENGINEERING

SIGNALLING

The Great Western established its signalling works at Caversham Road, Reading, in around 1859. The gradual expansion of the works saw almost all of the Great Western signalboxes and signalling equipment designed and built here. Between 1896 and 1910 the works were turning out some 150 signalboxes a year and by 1923 there were 2,066 signalboxes and 23,467 signals in use on the Great Western. After Nationalisation, the works continued to produce and repair signalling equipment for the Western Region, but by the early 1960s the Modernisation Plan was in full swing, with the old mechanical boxes being gradually replaced by new electric panel boxes. Maintenance took over from construction at Caversham and the works finally closed on 29 June 1984. The site is now covered by commercial buildings.

Above:
There were two boxes at Savernake: Savernake East and Savernake West. This picture shows Savernake West box on 27 April 1974. Built of brick and timber it contained a 32-lever frame and was opened *circa* 1884, and was closed on 19 November 1978. The concrete toilet was obviously a later addition. The box is facing the West of England main line which is in the foreground, while running behind the box is the remains of the branch to Marlborough. The line from Savernake to Marlborough Low Level was closed to passenger traffic on 11 September 1961 and to goods on 7 September 1964. *GWT/MY*

Right:
Bathampton Junction signalbox was opened on 21 September 1956, and replaced an earlier GW signal box that was closed on the same date. As can be seen, the box, which was fitted with a 52-lever frame, was a standard BR design in brick with a flat roof. It was closed on 17 August 1978.
CGS/GWT Collection

Bledlow signalbox was opened in November 1891 and was a standard Great Western brick and timber design, containing 15 levers. The box, which was situated on the Princes Risborough end of the single platform, is seen here as the 7.50am service from Oxford to Princes Risborough arrives on 25 August 1962. Passenger services were withdrawn from the branch on 7 January 1963, but this section, from Princes Risborough to Thame, remained open for oil traffic until September 1991. Bledlow box was closed some years earlier on 15 September 1965 and although it has long gone, the station building survives as a private house. *GWT/PAF*

Above:
A view looking west from the up platform at Kintbury, on 13 June 1974. On the right is Kintbury box, which contained a 20-lever frame and also controlled the adjacent level crossing. The box was opened in around 1884 and was rebuilt by the Great Western in 1947. It was closed during 1974. On the left is the down station starter signal, and on the right a brown and cream Western Region enamel 'Beware of Trains' sign. The large cast-iron station running-in board has been painted black with white lettering.
GWT/MY

Right:
'Western' Class 52 No D1036 *Western Emperor* speeds past Lavington signalbox on 7 September 1968 with the 06.50 service from Plymouth to Paddington. This box was opened in around 1900 and was fitted with a 29-lever frame. Constructed of brick and timber with a slate roof, it was closed on 22 January 1979. *GWT/PAF*

Above:
A fine array of starter and distant signals at Westbury station pictured here on 20 April 1976. In the centre is the large signalbox at Westbury North. This was constructed of brick with a slate roof and was opened by the Great Western in 1899. It was originally fitted with an 82-lever frame, but this was enlarged to 99 levers in November 1949. The entrance to the box was via a centre end stairway. The opening of a new power box at Westbury on 13 May 1984 and the introduction of multiple-aspect signalling (MAS), resulted in the closure of Westbury North box together with 12 others in the area. *GWT/MY*

Left:
A view from the east end of the up relief platform at Taplow shows the signalbox and goods sidings. This box replaced two earlier ones at Taplow East and West, and was opened on 30 June 1930. It contained a 71-lever frame and was constructed using a steel frame with concrete infills. The upper section is constructed of timber with a slate roof. Taplow box was closed on 20 July 1974 and has since been demolished. Standing in the East sidings are the yard shunter, '1600' class 0-6-0PT No 1622 and '6100' class 2-6-2T No 6117 which is ready to leave with the pick-up goods service to Hinksey yard, Oxford. *GWT/CGS*

Below:
A close-up of the signalbox at Cranmore, taken on 7 May 1966. This was a standard Great Western box built of brick and timber with a slate roof. Opened on 11 September 1904, it contained a 27-lever frame, and was closed on 19 May 1968. Passenger services over the Witham to Wells branch were withdrawn on 9 September 1963, and freight services ceased on 17 January 1966, but the line remained open as far as Cranmore for bitumen traffic until September 1985. The site at Cranmore was taken over by the East Somerset Railway during 1971 and was formally opened as a preserved line on 20 June 1975. The box still survives and is currently being restored to full operational condition, following a number of years' use by David Shepherd as an art gallery.
GWT/PAF

CRANMORE SIGNAL BOX

Above:
Ex-Great Western '4300' class 2-6-0 No 6342 stands at Morfa Mawddach signalbox with the 1.58pm service from Barmouth to Machynlleth on 1 June 1962. The box, which was built by the GWR, contained a 38-lever frame and was opened as Barmouth Junction in 1931. It was renamed Morfa Mawddach on 17 June 1960. The Ruabon to Barmouth line was closed on 18 January 1965 and the signalbox was closed shortly after this date. The Machynlleth to Barmouth and Pwllheli line is still operational and is today radio signalled. No 6342 was built at Swindon in March 1923 and withdrawn from service in September 1962. *PAF/GWT Collection*

Below:
A high-level viewpoint shows 'Western' Class 52 No D1038 *Western Sovereign* passing Bristol East Depot yard on its way out of the city with the 11.15 Bristol Temple Meads to Paddington service on 19 April 1969. Suspended on the side of the cutting is the former Bristol East Depot signalbox. This box, which contained a 69-lever frame, was constructed of wood and supported on iron girders. It was built in 1909 and was closed on 1 January 1960, being replaced by Bristol East Depot Main Line box. This contained a 90-lever frame and can just be seen at the bottom right of the picture. The opening of a new power box at Bristol resulted in the Main Line box being closed on 20 July 1970. *GWT/PAF*

Above:
The Western Region also inherited quite a number of pre-Grouping company boxes. Pictured here are two ex-Cambrian Railways examples. The first is the small box at Three Cocks Junction, which stood on the south end of the junction platform, and is seen here on

27 October 1963. Built by the Cambrian Railways and opened on 22 October 1890, it was constructed of brick and timber with a slate roof and contained a 40-lever Dutton Type 1 frame. Three Cocks Junction box was closed on 31 December 1962. *GWT/CGS*

Left:
The second Cambrian Railways example shows the signalbox at Newtown, Montgomery, on 23 June 1974. This was a much larger box, fitted with a 54-lever Dutton Type 3 frame, which was opened in around 1893. This box was also constructed of brick and timber with a slate roof, and has arched brick windows to the frame room, and there is a single-line pick-up apparatus alongside the box. With the introduction of radio signalling on the line, Newtown signalbox was closed on 21 October 1988. *GWT/MY*

Above:
The up advanced starter and Colthrop distant signals at Thatcham on 15 June 1974. Constructed at Caversham Road, the signals are mounted on a steel pole with a ladder and inspection platforms. *GWT/MY*

Right:
Down starter signals at West Ruislip, 23 June 1963, mounted on a steel support column with a single high-level inspection platform.*GWT/CGS*

Below:
Hamstead Crossing signalbox pictured on 27 July 1974. Hamstead Crossing is situated on the Berks and Hants line between Kintbury and Newbury. The box was a non-standard GW design and was opened on 9 February 1921. It was fitted with a nine-lever frame and also controlled the adjacent level crossing. It was closed on 17 April 1978. *MY/GWT Collection*

Left:
A wooden down home signal and signal post at Uffculme, Devon, on 17 August 1963. *GWT/MY*

Below:
The new and the old as an HST in InterCity 125 livery, speeds over the superb brick arches of Brunel's Thames Bridge at Maidenhead, on 19 March 1977. Opened on 1 July 1839, and a tribute to Brunel's design, the bridge is one of many listed structures on the Western Region. Today, nearly 30 years after their introduction, the HSTs (now Class 43) are being operated by the First Great Western franchise and still form the backbone of high-speed services over the old Great Western main lines. *GWT/MY*

SIGNALLING